GW00597844

20. OCT

How to Henparty

The Essential Guide

Kate Hyde

CURRACH
PRESS

First published in 2009 by
CURRACH PRESS
55A Spruce Avenue, Stillorgan Industrial Park, Blackrock, County Dublin
www.currach.ie
and
www.henparty.ie, Unit 5, Dunhill Enterprise Park, Dunhill,
County Waterford
1 3 5 4 2

Cover by bluett
Origination by Currach Press
Printed by ColourBooks, Baldoyle Industrial Estate, Dublin 13
ISBN: 978-1-85607-995-2
The author has asserted her moral rights.
Copyright © Kate Hyde 2009

ACKNOWLEDGEMENTS

First and foremost I would like to thank my husband, Paul, who has been my rock from the beginning. When henparties consumed every conversation in the house Paul never complained, but always encouraged and supported me. My parents Rom and Verna and my brother Jonathan have also been a huge driving force in my writing this book and I thank them also.

Thanks to my mother-in-law Elizabeth for her help and also to Helena Mulkearns. Thanks to Jo O'Donoghue and all the team at Currach Press for giving me the chance to publish *How to Henparty* and for being so lovely to work with.

A huge thank you to my 'dragons', Gavin Duffy and Niall O'Farrell, who have supported me throughout the writing of this book and beyond. A particular thank you to Gavin for all his help and encouragement.

Finally a special word of thanks to all the ladies who contributed their stories to the book and to all my friends who let me plan their henparties and inspired me to start my business and write this book. Without them none of this would have happened.

Kate Hyde, Waterford, July 2009

For My Mum, Verna

CONTENTS

INTRODUCTION

So you are getting married. The church is booked, the band is in place, the guest list is nearly there and your dress is en route to the bridal shop. There is only one thing left to do: organise your henparty. Love them or hate them, a bride's henparty is as integral to her wedding as the wedding dress itself. It is her last night of freedom before tripping down the aisle, bidding farewell to the single life and trading it all in for the man of her dreams. At this important event, the bride surrounds herself with her friends and family for the last time as a single woman. Old boyfriends are lamented, school pictures are produced and tears accompany laughter as stories are shared.

Henparties today are not just the 'couple of drinks and dancing' that they were in the past. It's no longer enough just to 'have a few' in the local pub, hit the nightclub and be home in bed for 2.00 am. Gone are the days of meeting the bride at the taxi rank and heading into town – along with the idea of limiting the occasion to a one-night affair. These days, the henparty is much more. Its structure has changed dramatically, with the focus being on a whole weekend away instead, with all the bells and whistles! Budgets are ignored, champagne is bought, activities are organised and the best restaurant in town is booked. When we say 'in town', needless to say, the town can be at the other end of the country or abroad. These days, henparties travel!

But where to start? Now that henparties are getting as competitive as weddings themselves, how do you, the maid of honour, know where to begin? What is the correct procedure when organising a henparty? Where do you go, what do you do, what will work and what won't? Should you ask the mothers or not? Should you have an afternoon activity or not?

The answers to these questions and more lie in this book. With a little bit of help, you can give the Hen the time of her life. The henparty today is as central to the success of the wedding as the rest of the proceedings. It can set the mood for the group when they meet again on the big day. There is no reason that the henparty you organise can't be the best yet. And after all, that's what it's all about.

> For my cousin's henparty, her dad sailed us around the harbour on their boat. I was really nervous, as I had never sailed before, but it was really good fun. The water was very calm and that helped. We had loads of champagne and her sister brought lots of nibbles for us as well. Everyone wore a black wig and a pink feather boa and we got some great pictures. The Hen had fairy wings and a pink curly wig. We had dinner in a nice restaurant that night. I remember one

girl needing to take an Alka Seltzer before we went dancing because she drank too much champagne on the boat!

Leonie

I didn't know about it but the girls planned a cooking lesson at a cooking school set up to accommodate parties like this. We all made our hors d'oeuvres, dinner and dessert and then the staff paired wine with everything. I walked around and joined all the stations so I got to chat with everyone. It was a great mixer for people who weren't acquainted with one another beforehand and a brilliant way to organise dinner. Afterwards we went out to a bar. It turned out to be a fabulous night and all the girls commented on what a great idea it was.

Linda

1

What Is a henparty?

Let's set the scene. A henparty is in essence a party for the bride before she marries. The bride-to-be, or 'Hen' as she is called, is joined by her closest female friends and family for a girls-only celebration. Henparties can take many shapes and forms but basically, there are five key henparty elements: an afternoon activity, a meal, games and dressing up, dancing and clubbing and an overnight or weekend stay in a hotel or special venue. There are of course many variations on this traditional model but celebration is at the core of any henparty: celebration, laughter, fun and friendship.

HENPARTY RULES
Like every time-honoured tradition, henparties involve a number of unspoken rules. These constitute 'the henparty way' and are guidelines that henparty novices should be aware of. The three core henparty rules are:

- Rule One: The Hen Always Gets What She Wants.

If the Hen decides everyone has to wear black wigs and jodhpurs, then everyone will happily wear black wigs and jodhpurs. If she decides everyone will go swimming in the sea in December, then everyone goes swimming in the sea in December. Saying no is not an option – what the Hen wants, she gets. To say 'woe betide the girl who doesn't comply' isn't even relevant because you do what you are told. End of story.

- Rule Two: You Must Go

You must go – but if you absolutely can't, you'd better have a very good reason. Not to go to a friend's henparty is like turning around and denouncing your friendship. Short of death, there is never a valid reason not to go to the henparty. Years of friendship have been leading up to this moment and not to go would undo them all.

- Rule Three: It's All about the Hen

The Hen must be the centre of attention at all times. To detract from this attention would be an unforgivable offence and most ladies are sharp enough to know what not to do. When the Hen is in the middle of the dance circle, you do not join her. When a group of guys are giving her send-off kisses, you do not vie for their attention. When the Hen drinks too much and starts telling the girls how much she loves them and cries, you do not mirror her behaviour. At all times it's all about the Hen.

THE HISTORY OF THE HENPARTY

The notion of the henparty originated with bachelor parties, or as they are more commonly called now, stag parties. As far back as the fifth century BC, in ancient Sparta, it is on record that men enjoyed dinners with their male counterparts before marriage, participating in activities of which a new bride would not have approved. These bachelor parties or stags have continued to this day, with the groom still participating in activities of which a bride would not approve.

While it was always a tradition to give the bride a send-off of sorts before her big day, it wasn't until the 1960s and the sexual revolution that the henparty as a separate concept began to emerge. Prior to this, women had kitchen parties or gatherings in relatives' houses. Often quiet, tame affairs, these send-offs remained the norm until the 1980s, when women started to get adventurous and began enjoying their last night of freedom as much as the men. They very quickly realised that there wasn't a single good reason they shouldn't – and so the henparty as we know it today was born.

The henparty is still evolving as a tradition, becoming more and more elaborate as it does. There is little doubt that the preparation that goes into a henparty today, and the level of celebration it generates, are every bit as wild and wonderful as the famed stag nights dreamed up by the lads.

Henparties take place all over the world. Tens of millions of women all around the globe party with their girlfriends before they trip down the aisle. In the US and Canada, brides have 'bachelorette parties', while the term 'henparty' is more common in Ireland, the UK, Australia and New Zealand. Canada also uses the term 'stagette', while the 'stag and doe party', a combination of men and women, is also taking off over there. This novel idea has yet to be adopted on this side of the world, since most of us still prefer to have our last night as single women without the men.

Scottish henparties are very similar to the Irish ones, with the exception of the Scottish tradition whereby the Hen walks through the pubs with a bucket in one hand and a kiss for the gentlemen in the other. The bucket serves to collect coins and notes – since yes, in Scotland the local men give the Hen money in exchange for a kiss on her Hen night. Some attractive brides have been known to make enough to pay for the wedding cake! This practice has yet to catch on in Ireland, with the real danger of single farmers on a mission invading the vicinity of Dublin's Temple Bar.

Polish henparties are called *Leánybúcsú* and, like Irish henparties, involve a nice meal in a restaurant. However these are held in the bride's home place and the party tends to stay in the restaurant for the night. They often organise a male dancer to entertain the ladies. In Hungary a henparty is called a *Polttarit* and is very similar to an Irish or English henparty. Ladies will typically go to their summer cottage or a spa, enjoying saunas and drinkies and pampering and dressing up the Hen, later heading off to the pub. Sounds familiar. But in order to give you a really clear impression of the idea behind the henparty, we thought we would include a few more personal testimonies of real events:

It is always fun going to a henparty – getting to know the Hen's other friends before the wedding is a plus for me. At one henparty I went to, we spent the morning sipping champagne and learned all about chocolates at a course the bride organised. We went on to make our own chocolates – the truffles were my personal favourites. Once they were made, we decorated them with even more chocolate and nuts. We packaged the chocolates that survived our munching into boxes and took them away with us.

The evenings and nights out are always good fun too. In particular, I love it when we play games or dares that everyone can be involved in. It's a great way of breaking the ice between the Hen's friends who don't know each other. I went to one henparty where we got the Hen out of the room for a bit and when she came back in we were all wearing T-shirts with a truly awful childhood photo on the front! Even the blow-up man doll had his own T-shirt!

Sally

The funniest thing I ever saw on a henparty was a male stripper. The bride had no idea he was coming and looked as if she was going to die. Her work friends organised the guy and he came to the holiday homes we were staying in before we went for dinner. He played 'King of my Castle' on a CD player and recited a poem about the bride. Then he stripped down to a thong. It was hilarious.

Katherine

I had a fantastic henparty but to be honest the one bad thing that comes into my mind when I look back is that two of my really close friends didn't come. I don't think they even realised how upset I was at the time. Both were friends from way back and top priority when I planned my guest list. One of them couldn't make it as she had booked a weekend away with her boyfriend and the other couldn't come because her husband was away and she didn't have a babysitter at the last minute. I don't think I really believed her!

Louise

It was about a week before the henparty that we (the two other bridesmaids and myself) began to realise that the maid of honour didn't really have anything planned. She was the bride's sister, so we assumed she had everything under control – until we realised that all she had really organised was the guest list, the restaurant and a few props for the dinner table. Another bridesmaid and I dug out some old photos of Lisa from school and made a scrapbook for her that we gave to her at the meal. Our other friend managed to organise a boat trip down the river on the Saturday afternoon and we brought some sparkling wine along which went down well. What was more annoying than anything was how the bride kept thanking her sister for organising the best henparty ever.

Brid

I had my henparty at the end of July 2008. I asked twenty of my friends and cousins but not my Mum, as I knew she wouldn't want to come. We went to a small town and I didn't have an activity planned but one of my best friends, unbeknownst to me, put a lot of work at the last minute into organising a surprise champagne lunch. The weather was divine and we sat outside sipping champagne and eating strawberries. My maid of honour had put a lot of thought into the night and she asked everyone to dress in black. Just before dinner we all had to put on bunny sets. It was so funny, I will never forget it. We had a fab meal in the restaurant in the hotel and then headed up the town to various pubs. The locals loved us. After that we went back to the hotel where there was a nightclub and we danced for hours. It was one of the best days of my life. I felt so loved!

Jen

2

Planning a Henparty

The first and foremost question for the person organising a henparty is where the party will be held. Would the Hen prefer a henparty abroad or at home? Many women would have little interest in a foreign henparty, so this option can be discounted immediately. But with the advent of low-cost travel and cheap package deals, travelling abroad for a henparty need not be the most expensive option. Low-cost carriers offer flights to every corner of Europe and, with a bit of planning, many of these destinations not only are great fun but competitive in terms of price.

Many women love the idea of having their henparties abroad – getting away from it all with their nearest and dearest and painting the town red, without the risk of bumping into neighbours or ex-boyfriends. Eastern Europe can be an ideal henparty location, with a little bit of effort. Accommodation, food and beer are all cheap and the price to get there and back need not be more than a coach ticket in Ireland or the price of the train from Cork to Dublin. Prague is the destination of choice for most henparties heading East.

The Spanish henparty is also a firm favourite, with many Irish and English women travelling to the Costas every year. Spain is famously inexpensive and there are many great deals to be had. Self-catering apartments are still the most popular choice, with night pubs and clubs charging a fraction of the admission price we pay in this country. Marbella and Madrid are two of the more popular henparty locations in Spain.

Mainland Europe need not be the only option. UK destinations are also extremely popular for Irish henparties, with many Hens heading to cities like Glasgow, Edinburgh and Liverpool for their big nights. Again, low-cost carriers have made these trips affordable and these destinations more accessible. As with a European henparty, having your henparty in the UK can be good value, with plenty of options in terms of accommodation and eating out.

WHO ORGANISES THE HEN?

It may seem like an odd question but be warned, this is an important point to clear up as early as possible when planning the henparty. Traditionally the maid of honour is the chief organiser and the only real input the bride has is to hand over her guest list, which we will deal with further on in the chapter. However, while many brides are happy to let their maids of honour plan the henparty, others may prefer to be mistresses of their own ships and plan the whole thing themselves. Either way, it is important to establish who is running the show, so that nothing is left to chance and the event is planned properly.

For a traditional henparty, the maid of honour typically receives a list of names and phone numbers or email addresses from the Hen. The Hen also tells the maid of honour where in the country or abroad she would like to go. At this point, the maid of honour contacts all the ladies on the list and tells them where and when the fun is happening. Those who know at this early stage that they won't be able to make the henparty will let the maid of honour know, while the rest send a little courtesy message to say that they got the text/email and are looking forward to the big night. This message will be something along the lines of: 'Thanks, Jane, looking forward to it. Anything I can do to help, just let me know.' The 'anything I can do to help' is a key part of the early return texts/emails.

At this point, the maid of honour tells the bride who definitely can't make it at this early stage. This can be a delicate process that requires tact and an ability to finesse the truth. Often there can be serious consequences if the reason for a refusal given doesn't include open-heart surgery or a prepaid luxury holiday for which a refund cannot be obtained. If a bride wants a large henparty and the maid of honour finds that the number of acceptances is turning out low, she should at this point revise the guest list, so that other friends who did not make the first guest list may be reconsidered and a second round of 'keep the date free' messages goes out.

Around this time, the bride very often bows out completely and the maid of honour takes charge of all things henparty: the accommodation, activities if any, dressing up ideas, finances and gifts. The bride has nothing more to do with proceedings, except for picking a fabulous outfit and turning up for the girls' night out of her dreams.

It is always and we stress *always*, a good idea for the bride to make sure that her maid of honour is up to the job. There are stories aplenty of brides who, at the eleventh hour, realised there was nothing planned for their henparty and hastily had to arrange activities and accommodation themselves.

There are stories of friends realising at the last minute that nothing had been organised by the maid of honour, requiring a belated scramble to make sure that all the stops were pulled out for the Hen. Ironically, it can often be sisters who slacken off coming up to the big event. It is unforgivable for a maid of honour to be lazy or indifferent. The bride should be aware that choosing the right maid of honour, if at all possible, will make life much easier.

While it may seem extraordinary, it can often happen that the bride is not in a position to choose the maid of honour she actually wants. She may be under heavy pressure to choose the maid of honour expected of her. A bride may feel obliged to choose a sister, a close friend or a cousin for the sake of the greater good. This, in turn, means that a bride can't always pick the person she knows will get the job done. While we would urge all brides to think carefully before they hand over organisational responsibility to someone with a tendency towards chaos or indifference, we also appreciate that in many situations it just cannot be avoided.

In the event that you do feel obliged to appoint a

maid of honour you know in your heart isn't up to the challenge, don't worry. This is a common situation and easily rectified. A quiet word in another bridesmaid's ear, or that of a sister or a close friend, will ensure the henparty is a success. Make sure this other designated person has a list of guests and phone numbers and can keep a close eye on proceedings at all times. As the bride, you can still remain out of the loop in terms of organising the henparty, while at the same time you can rest assured that even if your maid of honour is a hopeless case, there is someone on the sidelines ready to save the day.

It can also happen that the bride will prefer to organise her own henparty from start to finish, looking for little or no help from the maid of honour or her bridesmaids. These Hens will choose the hotels, the restaurants, invite the guests and plan the games. Many Hens go so far as to print T-shirts for all their guests with the text or pictures of their choice. Some have gone so far as to keep the event's proceedings a secret from the majority of their guests. Yes, these Hens do exist! And while for many of you reading this book these women may come across as maniacal control freaks who clearly are marrying men who like a 'spirited woman', it is very often the case that the Hen simply wants to be in control herself. If you are the maid of honour for a woman like this, our advice is to let her go. Trying to organise a henparty for a woman who likes organising things herself is going to be an exhausting and trying experience. Smile and nod when she asks you what you think of her plans and apart from the odd 'Do you need me to do anything?' just stay in the background and look good.

Other tried and tested methods for organising a henparty include having all the bridesmaids organise the henparty, or a group of sisters. This can be an ideal situation, in that no one person is solely responsible for the success, or failure, of the event. The jobs are divided up equally and everyone has an input. Where this plan falters, of course, is when personalities clash, or if there is a power struggle. Bitching and fighting will invariably result in bad feeling that can last way beyond the wedding. So if you, as the Hen, are choosing a group to take care of proceedings, choose a group that will work well together and whose members aren't liable to kill each other.

WHO TO ASK AND HOW MANY
This is the eternal henparty question. No sooner is the ring on a bride's finger and the date for the wedding set than she starts planning the henparty. With the exception of the guest list for her wedding, it is one of the most critical guest lists a young lady will ever write. For those who make it on to that list, it is a symbol of being in 'the inner circle', 'the chosen few', 'the friend for life'.

Even if the henparty guests number more than forty people, it is still an honour to be invited, as it means you are worthy. For this reason, the bride will always pick selectively and justify every name on the list, all with a small commentary. Nobody is on the list by accident, everyone earns their place – from the front runners to the number-builders. Even the most obvious choices will be justified with a small tag: 'Lisa, Joan, Margaret and Sarah of course,' or, 'Mary and Joanne I know since school, it's a no-brainer.'

Those further down the list demand a little more justification. 'If I don't ask Lucy, that's our friendship over,' or, 'Well, Laura asked me to hers so I have to ask her to mine, really.' Likewise, those who don't make the grade warrant explanations for their omission. 'She didn't ask me to hers, I have no intention of asking her to mine,' and, 'If I ask Jane there will be tension between her and Pauline and I am not having tension at my henparty.'

The size of the henparty should always be well thought out. Some brides choose to ask cousins; others do not. Some brides ask the girls from work; again, others do not. But there are no hard and fast rules when the Hen is writing the henparty guest list. Some ladies prefer the idea of an intimate henparty, with six or eight very close sisters, cousins or friends creating a feeling of the select few. Some feel a large henparty can be seen as vulgar or crass, while others simply don't want a huge gang trailing around the town together. A small henparty usually means that everyone is already acquainted, so the bride doesn't have to worry about silly things like people bonding. Instead, all attention can be lavished on her. Shy brides are particularly fond of small henparties for obvious reasons, as are brides who don't really want a lavish henparty but still want to mark the occasion.

Small henparties can be great but they can also have their disadvantages. A very small henparty can lack atmosphere in a large restaurant or pub and if all the guests already know each other, there may not be too much variety in terms of conversation. Six women dressed like giant Playboy bunnies are also a little less effective than fifteen women in the same gear.

One benefit of a very large henparty is that it can give a girl a sense of popularity and power. To be the Hen on a henparty of thirty women means that a lot of ladies will be pandering to your every whim. For a bride who loves attention, it can be heaven. The bride gets to decide what all these women wear, where they all go to drink, what kind of restaurant they eat in – and even when they get to go to bed!

Then there are brides who invite every single female they know and end up with an enormous henparty. Some just don't want to leave anyone out and have a 'more the merrier' approach. When justifying names on the list (remember they are always justified), the bride won't have a little story for each person but instead simply notes, 'Ah yes, of course, Martha' or, 'Oh yeah… and Sandra.' Everyone is invited!

The problem with a large henparty is that when you bring twenty-plus women together who don't know each other, one of two things can happen. Firstly, they can all immediately dislike each other for no good reason and vicious bitching can begin that may continue until the wedding. Secondly, schisms can emerge with the 'work gang' on one side of the dance floor and the 'girls from school' on the other. For a Hen, who may have to decide which gang she will 'YMCA' with, this can be tough.

The average number on a henparty in the Noughties seems to be around twelve to fifteen people. This number usually comprises a few relatives, a few from school, a few from college and, you guessed it, a few from work. A few from each group lessens the risk of having massive groups within the henparty and also encourages the ladies to mix. Schisms are less likely and while there is a nice number of ladies on the dance floor with the Hen, she isn't liable to lose half of them to another floor of the nightclub or a rugby team downstairs. In essence, there is control. There is the right level of popularity, coupled with the ability to spot at twenty paces whether there has been an escape from the group or a refusal to wear the rabbit's ears.

Mothers, Mothers-in-Law and Older Relatives
One age-old problem that will probably continue long into the next century is the question of whether to ask the mothers of the bride and groom on the henparty. For years, brides have agonised over the decision, wanting to keep themselves and everyone else happy. It can be a decision made easily but just as frequently it is one that requires the negotiation skills of a highly trained diplomatic operative.

There are some mothers who would never want to go on their child's henparty and to whom the idea would not even occur. These mothers just button up their cardies, sip their tea and tell the bride to behave and not drink too much on the trip. Being unable even to imagine what they would do on a henparty, they look forward instead to their daughter coming home and telling them all about it.

To have a mother like this on a henparty will not only mean certain death for the atmosphere, it will probably mean certain death for the mother whose heart may give out as the night moves up a gear. A conservative mother will never thank you for asking her to your henparty because you felt guilty, only to be asked to hold the blow-up man as your friend uses the loo. She really does not want to be privy to the sordid details of your college love life before you met the man of your dreams. She has no real desire to watch her baby shimmying to Beyoncé on the dance floor and screaming when 'Rhythm is a Dancer' comes on.

Readers with conservative mothers, please take our advice. Guilt is not a reason to ask your mother to your henparty. Guilt is what you will feel when your mother has to be sedated by paramedics.

On the other hand, there are mothers who are absolutely up for the henparty. They have their outfits picked and are ready for road. These mothers will laugh as loudly as the rest of your friends when you pinch that guy's ass for a dare. These mothers will go drink for drink with the girls and dance with the best of them to Madonna's 'Like a Prayer'. These mothers wouldn't miss their daughter's last night of freedom for anything and are more than able to hold their own with the younger women. These mothers really can pull it off – and if readers have mothers like this, we absolutely encourage them to ask them along. What better bonding could a mother have than a night out with all the girls before her own little girl walks down the aisle?

It must also be noted, however, that just because a mother is up for a henparty and can talk the talk, it doesn't mean that it is the right choice for you. You may not want to ask your mother or mother-in-law on your henparty. You may be confident that your mother will be able to handle the fun and games but you yourself may not be ready to see her slamming back a Tequila. Many brides-to-be have not seen the crazy party side of their mothers and they may not want to. This is OK too! At the end of the day this is *your* big event and you get only one henparty, so take some time and think it through. Having a substitute night for mothers and older relatives is an excellent way to resolve this tricky situation. A 'kitchen party' is an excellent idea for keeping everyone happy and we will discuss that option further in Chapter 12.

Men

There are ladies in our midst who often consider asking men to their henparties. Some ladies out there have life-long male friends and wonder whether they should ask them to come along and dance the night away. Think about it carefully, ladies. Our experience tells us there are more minuses than pluses to this idea.

Where a group of ladies are sharing intimate stories of their past love lives they may not feel comfortable talking about them in front of a man – no matter how 'cool' you think he is. They may not feel comfortable shimmying with him on the dance floor or asking him what he is wearing to the wedding. No man wants to hear what kind of bikini wax the bride is getting for the big day or chat about how soon she may have babies. What man wants to hear 'hilarious' stories of wedding night difficulties, removing corsets and all-in-ones. In our experience, no man really wants to be on a henparty.

The beauty of a friendship with a man is that even if you don't ask him, he won't hold it against you forever, or tell all the others that he is really hurt and doesn't know if he can go to the wedding. Men are easy and will know why they weren't invited. So our advice is: for everyone's sake, have a separate night out with the boys.

3

WHERE TO GO?

Deciding where to go and what kind of henparty to have is as easy or as difficult as you make it. Take our advice and don't over-think it. The location is important but factors such as who you bring and what you do will count even more towards making the henparty a roaring success. So long as the girls are in tow and ready to party, the location should be secondary. Nevertheless, there are some points worth considering when choosing your henparty destination.

THE CITY
Many Hens opt for bright lights and big city. Going to a major city is still a very popular choice for henparties and there is a lot to be said for the lure of the big smoke. In terms of choice, a city centre henparty affords more pubs, clubs and restaurants and no matter what time of the year, you are always guaranteed a good atmosphere and plenty of people out and about. Different budgets are also much easier to cater for. If you opt for a cheap and cheerful henparty you will have more choice in terms of accommodation and eating out. Similarly,

if you are planning on blowing the budget, there are plenty of options to choose from. High-end hotels and restaurants are easily found.

For henparties that have a mixed age group, a city henparty is a good idea. The variety that goes with the city means that guests aren't restricted to one activity. Take, for example, an occasion for which the maid of honour has organised a belly-dancing class in the city centre and everyone is invited. Having the henparty in a city means that mothers and aunts in the group can find a spa or hit the department stores, while the younger guests have a few cocktails and learn how to shake those hips. Similarly, if a day of shopping is planned or a stroll around town, those who prefer to have a couple of drinks and get in the party mood instead of hitting the stores can do so without any difficulty. City centre henparties simply mean choice.

The disadvantages of a city centre henparty are just as important to consider. The more pubs and nightclubs there are, the more potential there is for guests to get lost. This is a common complaint of city centre henparties. A guest may meet a rugby player in the first pub, fall in love and go missing in action. Or two guests might stop to buy cigarettes, promising to catch up, and are never seen again – until breakfast next morning, at least. If you have a very large henparty it can be difficult to keep tabs on everyone and make sure they are present right until the end of the night. If the Hen is liable to become upset at losing bodies along the way, a city henparty is not a good option for her.

Likewise, with a city henparty, there is the real and

present danger of bumping into another party. We've all seen it: fifteen women in one corner dressed as cowboys, fifteen women in the other dressed as devils. Two henparties, one dance floor – it's a bloodbath waiting to happen. If a Hen couldn't care less whether she is the only Hen in town, this won't be an issue but if the Hen is looking forward to being the be-all and end-all, a city-centre location is not worth considering.

THE TOWN
The small town henparty certainly has its merits. There is a lot to be said for rolling into a town and taking it over for the weekend. The choice of pubs and restaurants may not be as extensive as with a city-centre henparty but there are always two or three henparty-friendly eateries to choose from and a number of options in terms of accommodation. In a town that may not have a huge tourist trade or strong economy, you are more likely to find decent hotel rates and inexpensive dinners, compared to city locations. Businesses will be delighted to see fifteen or twenty women arrive into town, looking to spend money on hotels, meals and alcohol.

Small towns can also be more intimate than larger henparty venues. Everyone stays together and even if they separate for half an hour, it is easy to reunite the group. Guests are less likely to go missing in a location that has a more limited selection of pubs and where visiting rugby teams are less likely to be on the tear. The henparty tends to travel from place to place as one group as opposed to splitting into several groups, something that can happen in a city.

Nightclubs and pubs in small towns are also more tolerant of henparties and access isn't normally a issue. Smaller towns tend to look at henparties more with bemusement than with the intolerance that can be found in larger towns or cities. Restaurants, bars and nightclubs are generally glad of the henparty's business – and glad of the extra men who will appear once they hear that a henparty is in full swing. On top of this, for the Hen who wants her party to be the only show in town, this is more likely to happen in a smaller location.

Of course small towns also have their disadvantages. Girls who are used to socialising in the bigger cities may feel claustrophobic and may not handle the lack of choice very well. In addition, the range of afternoon activities may be limited, or it may not be possible to arrange an afternoon activity at all. It is also worth noting that not all towns are suitable for henparties and it is necessary to make enquiries before a henparty is booked. Some towns may have a very large population but no nightclub. This is something that the maid of honour could easily overlook when organising a henparty.

THE VILLAGE

Don't knock them until you have tried them: village henparties are slowly but surely becoming something of a cult. If the Hen doesn't want to take the risk that there might be another henparty nearby and wants to make sure everyone stays together all night, the village henparty is for her.

Of course not every village will be suitable for a henparty. Many will only have one or two pubs, nowhere to go dancing, one Chinese restaurant and a chipper. But there are villages out there that are perfect for henparties. Some even have a party reputation, a late bar or a small quirky hotel that serves into the early hours. There are villages to which punters come from miles around and where late on a Saturday night, all the young and not so young folk come out in their droves to cut loose. These little gems are the villages you need to locate for your henparty.

Seaside villages that have a strong sailing community can be perfect for this type of henparty. At certain times of the year, a village with one pub and two restaurants can be the best place in the country. That's where you might find groups of yachtsmen having a few pints on the street outside the pub, burger vendors nearby, one man and his guitar in the corner and house parties aplenty only dying for a group of celebrating women to drop by. Other villages have summer festivals that bring people in from all over the hinterland for the weekend. An amazing atmosphere, created by bunting, merry-go-rounds and dodgy candy-floss stalls – all in terribly bad taste but great fun – makes for something different from the norm. Self-catering accommodation is ideal for a small village henparty and once the party in the village is over, it can continue back at the house, free from the constraints of the noise limits in a hotel residents' bar.

While we enthusiastically advocate village henparties, of course we must also point out their shortcomings. Village henparties are not for a girl who cannot live without Brown Thomas being no more than twenty minutes away, or for the girl who goes to pieces without reception on her i-phone. Don't even consider having a village henparty if you are bringing guests who may recoil in fear at the sight of a muck savage (local farmer) or remove their Christian Louboutin shoes on the off-chance that a heel would get stuck in something nasty on the street. There is simply no point.

The other downside to a village henparty is the problem of accommodation. Villages like those I have described are only worth visiting during their busy season but this is when rooms will be at a premium, either very expensive or impossible to get. Forward planning is crucial for a party like this, in order to avoid paying top dollar or taking the risk of everything being booked out.

> For my best friend's wedding, I organised her hen night in a village by the sea. I think that it's the henparty that we're all still talking about – by far. It was a beautiful summer's day and we all went for a swim on the beach when we got there. We did the usual meal thing in the only hotel in the village and then went to both bars dressed as cowgirls. At the end of the night, we were invited to the afters of a fortieth birthday party in a house in the village. By the time we left the next morning, we were practically members of the community. I would never have a city henparty when I get married myself after that craic.
>
> *Mary*

> The worst henparty I was ever at was in London. We went for the weekend and it cost an arm and a leg.

There were ten of us and nobody knew the city well enough to find our way around. We had a lovely meal early in the evening but after that it went downhill fast. They wouldn't let us into several of the clubs we went to and, although everybody was trying to make the best of it, things just kept going wrong – and on top of everything, it was raining cats and dogs. It really would have made all the difference if we had put a bit of thought into making some proper bookings ahead of time.

Deirdre

4

What Kind of Henparty?

This may seem like an obvious question but there is so much choice on the market these days in terms of henparties that it is worth considering all options, especially if the Hen wants a henparty to remember.

Here are some of our favourites:

THE TRADITIONAL HENPARTY
The old reliable, this henparty model has been serving women well for decades. There are five key elements to the traditional henparty. First comes an afternoon activity, which we will explore in detail in Chapter 5. This is followed by a meal in a nice restaurant or hotel, with all the girls getting glammed up for dinner and plenty of wine on the table. After the meal, the maid of honour dresses up the bride and everyone in the group puts on their henparty gear. At this stage of proceedings henparty games are played and the bride is suitably shamed. The next stage sees the group going on to some local pubs and clubs and the fifth and final stop for the henparty is the accommodation. Hotels, B&Bs, guest houses and self-catering facilities are the most popular

options. The traditional henparty typically lasts from one to two nights.

THE MUSIC FESTIVAL HENPARTY
One new style of henparty that is beginning to take off is a bash that takes place at a music festival. With more and more festivals coming on stream each year, the festival henparty is starting to prove very popular, especially for ladies who aren't into the 'traditional' henparty with a night of cocktails and Bon Jovi. Music festivals are perfect for a gang of girls who want to have the craic, without the pomp and ceremony of the typical henparty. In other words no dressing up, no games, no tiaras – and most importantly – no cheesy nightclubs. Instead you'll enjoy camp fires, good bands, beer tents and like-minded music lovers to dance with till dawn. Check out festival websites for ideas on where to go and upcoming festivals in Ireland and the UK, Spain and Eastern Europe.

THE SPA HENPARTY
For the Hen who doesn't want the tack and garishness of a traditional henparty but would still like to mark the event, the spa weekend is becoming increasingly popular. 'Tacky' and 'common' are the words that spring to this lady's mind when she thinks of a henparty and since vulgarity and unnecessary boisterousness will do nothing for her reputation, the obvious replacement is a spa weekend. What could be nicer than sipping a vodka martini while waiting for Inge to massage the week's tension away from your shoulders? After all, stress

takes its toll on every busy career woman in the rat race. Many spa resorts are now delighted to offer weekends to henparties and many excellent locations and packages are available.

THE CAMPING HENPARTY

Opting for a henparty in a circle of tents might sound like a most unappealing option for any henpartier hell-bent on an evening of champers, nibbles and wine. On closer inspection, however, we can see that camping is becoming an increasingly popular henparty choice. Even for the most seasoned social butterflies, camping henparties are catching on fast and developing something of a cult status. For the outdoorsy type, a campfire in the wild with a couple of cans of beer, ready meals and a tent are enough. However, in the competitive social culture we have become accustomed to, ladies are now bringing the makings of Bellinis along with them on camping henparties. When you want to rough it but still look your best and spoil the Hen, strawberries and champers, luxury sleeping bags and Marks and Spencers finest for lunch the next day are the way to go.

THE ARTISTIC HENPARTY

Organising a henparty around pottery-making, art classes, cookery weekends or millinery workshops can provide excellent possibilities for women who would prefer something with a bit of creativity for their henparty instead of a 'knees-up'. Many centres around the country provide all-day events with recommended or inclusive accommodation for such a party. These days or weekends away are becoming a popular alternative for more mature Hens, or henparties with older participants and non-drinkers. You'll be surprised at how many of your friends have been 'meaning to do something like that for ages' and will react with delight to find you've finally organised it for them – and thrown in a party to boot.

THE OUTDOORSY HENPARTY

For groups of friends that include strong, sporty women up for a challenge, then there are plenty of outdoor activity centres around the country that will be delighted to host your henparty. Dormitories, communal kitchens and contraband wine are the order of the day. These weekends can be immensely good fun and are definitely something out of the ordinary. The majority of these centres will cater for everybody from the hardened hockey player right down to the book-loving, sport-hating novice, so nobody should be under any pressure to take part in activities they aren't comfortable with. While not being as far removed from luxury as camping, there is still a feeling of the 'great outdoors' in a henparty of this type and for a group of good friends, these weekends can be incredibly good craic. The outdoorsy henparty comes highly recommended.

THE SHOPPING HENPARTY

Pretty self explanatory, the shopping henparty is designed for ladies who love to spend! So flex the credit card, take a deep breath and hit the stores as the shopping henparty takes off in this country. Some limo companies will even go so far as to pick up and drop off the gang, with champagne provided en route to get everyone in the spirit. Ladies hit the stores for a few hours, followed by a hairdo and a set of new nails in a nearby salon. Many hairdressers are now targeting henparties for bookings and will provide cocktails and champagne as you get your hair and nails done for the big night ahead. This is a sporty girl's worst nightmare and best suited to ladies who 'like to lunch'.

I don't know how everyone else feels but I am beginning to get tired of henparties. It's always the same thing – going to a town, having dinner and ending up in a club. It's not even that I don't like henparties, I just hate the fact they are all the same. Especially considering these days, with the economic climate, I think less is more. In other words – if we can start thinking of interesting alternatives to expensive extravaganzas, then all the better. My mates took me on a 'Celtic pilgrimage' to Newgrange – we all went there, took photos around the stones, sat out in the open air on the grass and told stories and then (well, OK – it has to be said), we went down to the local pub for a well-earned pint. It was brilliant – really unusual and I didn't miss bunny tails one bit.

Saoirse

There is a music festival on in Slovakia every year with really high-class acts. It's pretty cheap to get tickets and I've been thinking of it for my henparty if I can get some cheap air fares. My brother-in-law has been there and told me it's really cheap over there, so it might be something a bit different to do if the price is right. Since it's a place you would never think of ordinarily, it will be a trip to remember. And camping at the festival will be an amazing experience.

Jane

5

AFTERNOON ACTIVITIES

Over the past four or five years, afternoon activities have become a key element on henparties. Prior to that, henparties generally began at dinner with guests arriving early in the evening or even meeting the henparty at the restaurant. Today things are different and, bearing in mind that henparties are now more of a weekend away than an evening out, afternoon activities are becoming a more important and permanent part of the henparty as we know it.

WHY AN AFTERNOON ACTIVITY?
Afternoon activities can be pivotal to the success of the henparty. To begin with, they are excellent ice-breakers. For a Hen having a big group, there will invariably be guests who don't know each other, or even ladies who don't know anyone but the Hen. For these guests the afternoon activity is a bit like team-building at work. Everyone feels a bit awkward at the beginning and nobody wants to stand out, but by the end of it, everyone is great pals and firm friendships have been made for the night ahead.

At a two-night henparty, one advantage to an afternoon activity is that it provides a focal point to the middle of the day. If the henparty is being held over two days, hanging around the hotel or holiday home all day while waiting to head off to the pub later can be tedious. An afternoon activity clears the head, breaks up the afternoon and provides a useful corrective to the temptation of starting alcohol consumption too early.

Another advantage is that expectant mothers, older relatives and younger guests can participate in the henparty, without having to sit through the torture of a drink-soaked meal. Older relatives might be uncomfortable in a pub and younger ones might be under-age. Many ladies have friends who, for one reason or another, can't make an evening party, so an afternoon activity allows them to enjoy part of the festivities without needing to commit time to the full event.

For a Hen who wants to stand out from the crowd, the afternoon activity can also be a fantastic method of showing all her friends how it is done. Ladies have been known to go to great lengths to out-do one another when choosing afternoon activities: the more elaborate and extraordinary the better. So if you are determined to hold the henparty to beat all others, a truly wonderful afternoon activity is a must, dahling!

WHY YOU SHOULD NOT HAVE AN AFTERNOON ACTIVITY

Afternoon activities also have their disadvantages. A few points should be considered when choosing your afternoon event, cost being first and foremost. Yes, we know it is your big moment. Yes, we know it's all about you this weekend and, yes, we also know we are going to have to sell a body organ to fund the three-hour thalassotherapy spa package you have booked for the afternoon. Keep it real, ladies. If you know your friends can afford the helicopter, book it and enjoy the harbour tour. But be mindful of friends who simply don't have the surplus cash, who could be in an extremely awkward position if asked to pay for elaborate adventures. Even the most reasonable afternoon activity can put financial strain on guests, so bear this in mind when choosing.

You should also consider your type of guest when choosing an afternoon activity. If you are in your mid-forties and having a henparty, it's possible that your friends won't be interested in paintballing or bungee-jumping. Likewise, if you are a young Hen with wild and crazy friends, asking them to attend a cookery demo is perhaps not the best plan. Just think it through.

Don't forget to take the location into account when deciding on an afternoon activity. If you have set your heart on water sports, don't pick a landlocked town.

There are many afternoon activities that are suitable for henparties and as the henparty industry grows, there are far more choices to cater for all tastes. Below you'll find some of the old favourites as well as some more recent fads.

AFTERNOON ACTIVITIES – OUTDOOR
Paintball
An oldie but a goodie, the paintball afternoon is still a roaring success with henparties around the country.

It's fast, it's fun and it's a great way to get the group to bond and lose their inhibitions. The group is split into two teams and both teams are given guns with paintballs. The losers are the team that is covered in the most paint at the end of the game. The players who start out shy are very often the ones who are roaring orders by the end of the game. The other advantage of this choice of afternoon activity is that paintball centres are located near most major cities and towns and even out in the countryside, so it should never be too difficult to find one. It's a great workout before a big meal for the calorie-conscious and ideal for an outdoorsy group. Paintball centres are easily found online or in telephone directories. Always check whether the centre is covered by insurance and make sure you are given the correct safety gear before playing.

Horse-riding
Although trendier activities may be tempting, many henparties still go horse-riding for their afternoon activity. Many ladies turn up their noses at the thought of something so traditional, yet this afternoon activity is regularly booked for henparties around the country. If you are 'hot to trot', horse-riding is the afternoon activity for you. Responsible stables will provide safety hats and even boots for guests who don't bring their own. All levels are generally catered for but when you are booking, it is worth mentioning whether the riders are experienced or novices – or a mixture. Find a horse-riding centre in the telephone directory or contact the local tourist office: they will usually have a list of schools.

After that it's a simple case of 'tally ho'.

Canoeing
Team activities are consistently popular with henparties and canoeing is one of the favourites. Canoeing is an inexpensive but fun way to spend a couple of hours in the afternoon. What better way to spend time with your friends than paddling around the coast with the sea beneath you and the wildlife around you? For the more adventurous, or seasoned paddlers, a river trip is a popular alternative, as is a session in a harbour playing games in the canoes. Outdoor pursuit centres are scattered throughout the country, many near towns and cities, and you can also find them in locations that aren't near the sea but have access to water. They can be easily located online. Canoeing is also a cost-effective afternoon activity, making it even more appealing.

Quad biking
Quad biking is another firm henparty favourite and as with paintball and horse-riding, there are quad bike centres located all around the country. Find them online or contact the local tourist office for names of centres in the area. For those of you who aren't familiar with the concept, quad bikes are like motorbikes but with four wheels. Instead of accelerating with a pedal, the rider controls acceleration by means of a switch on the handlebars. The quad bikes are all-terrain vehicles, which allows them to travel over mounds, through streams and across muddy fields. It's a fast, fun and dirty activity. A quad centre will usually provide a one-and-a-half-hour

class for the group. They'll first be shown how to use the bikes, then brought around an obstacle course and let loose. Quad bikes are great for a mixed age group, as riders can travel as fast or as slowly as they like. It's also a relatively inexpensive afternoon activity for the amount of fun it will provide. Once nobody breaks a nail of course...

Sailing Courses

For those who have often thought of trying their luck on a yacht, an afternoon sailing course can not only be great fun but can be the start of a love affair with the ocean. Very often sailing is deemed an elitist sport, the preserve of the rich and famous. In reality, it is more accessible than you think. Taking a sailing lesson as part of your henparty will show you and your friends the basics and who knows – you may even enjoy it. If you are travelling to a seaside location, make some enquiries and find out if there is a yacht club or sailing school in the area. This information should be available online or any friend who sails should be in the know about clubs around the coast that offer courses. Then it's just a matter of booking the boat. You will learn the basics and all the key sailing terms – from 'navigation' to 'knots'. Just bring a warm jumper.

AFTERNOON ACTIVITIES – PAMPERING

Spa Sessions

For the Zsa Zsa Gabor girls among you whose idea of sport is getting your nails done, a spa afternoon is the thing for you. In this day and age, most large towns and cities have spa facilities, or beauticians with several rooms who will provide the service. Check online or look up the local telephone directory. Many spas have packages for henparties and will give you the run of the establishment. Enjoy masks, mud baths, seaweed wraps and massages. Relax, unwind and take some time out of the rat race. Forget the hustle and bustle of nine to five and treat yourself to an afternoon of pampering and indulgence. After all, it's your henparty and you're worth it.

Wine-tasting

Can you think of a nicer way to spend an afternoon than sipping a variety of reds and enjoying some mature cheese as you do? Wine-tasting classes are firm favourites for henparties these days, with more and more companies offering the service. Some will hold the session on their premises; others will come to your house or base and bring the all-important wines and cheeses with them. Ask a local wine shop if they know anyone in the area who gives classes. Many course providers now advertise online, so check the Internet too. Wine-tasting doesn't require the heave-ho of an outdoor activity but still gives ladies an opportunity to mingle, chat and get to know each other before the night ahead. It is a very civilised afternoon activity and one that discerning ladies will enjoy. Once everyone remembers to spit their wine and not get trollied...

Makeup Parties

Another afternoon favourite, the makeup party, is fast becoming the activity of choice for the 'glam' henparty. A trained make-up artist or beautician will come to your house, or host the afternoon at their premises. Ring a local beauty salon and ask them if they can recommend someone, or check online as many make-up artists now have websites. The norm is for guests to bring their own makeup and learn how to apply it correctly. The makeup artist will show you how to define your eyes, maximise your lips or perfect the smoky look for a big night out. Let her show you the tricks of the trade – how to hide those black bags and cover those spots. She will often go around to all the ladies and have a good root in their makeup bags, telling them what to keep and what should have been thrown away years ago. This can be a great pampering and informative afternoon and after all, every girl likes an opportunity to learn how she can improve her appearance.

AFTERNOON ACTIVITIES – CREATIVE

Pottery-making

Many arts and crafts centres have begun to host henparties and will be delighted to welcome you and your guests for an afternoon of pottery-making. Call the local tourist office or look up the online arts listings in the area you have chosen to see if there are any centres in the locality. For ladies who are neither outdoorsy nor 'girlie girls', a pottery class is an excellent choice. Everybody bonds, friendships are forged and vases are made for the mantelpiece. Pottery centres will provide all the necessary tools for the afternoon and will usually supply refreshments. They will show you how to work the clay, how to throw it on the wheel and how to get it ready for the furnace. Some have also been known to turn a blind eye to the odd bottle of wine being smuggled in the back door.

Millinery
For something completely different, why not learn how to make a hat at your henparty? You can schedule a millinery course for your afternoon activity. All materials are provided and experts in their field will guide guests through the hat-making process. It's a very creative afternoon and the idea behind henparty classes is that guests make a hat for the wedding itself and wear it on the big day. Millinery classes are more expensive than other afternoon activities but ideal for small groups or to make sure that yours is a henparty with a difference. Finding a milliner who caters for this kind of event can be quite a challenge but it's worth checking online to see if there are any in the area you have chosen for your henparty.

AFTERNOON ACTIVITIES – KEEP FIT

Bellydancing Classes
Yes, you heard right – bellydancing classes. There are classes located all over the country and many will provide the bellydancing costumes necessary to get into the spirit of the art. What could be funnier then learning how

to swing your hips, jiggle your love handles and get to know how the ladies of the Orient have charmed their men for millennia. Bellydancing teachers will often offer other forms of dance with the class, including burlesque and hula. The Internet is the best source to find these classes, as well as word of mouth. Classes typically last an hour or two and have the added benefit of providing a great workout. An inexpensive and hilarious afternoon activity, bellydancing comes highly recommended.

Pole-dancing

Pole-dancing classes are another exceptionally entertaining choice. You can find several companies offering classes online and it shouldn't be hard to find one near you. One-off afternoon pole-dancing classes are becoming more and more common for henparties and contrary to popular belief, it is not as seedy as it sounds. A good pole-dancing teacher will show you how to perform a range of beginner moves and how to put them altogether into a routine. The end result is hysterical! Also, contrary to popular opinion, you do not have to wear spandex and knee-high boots. Unless you want to, of course. A pole-dancing class is one of the best keep-fit sessions you can take while laughing. It's no wonder that several celebrities have had poles installed in their homes. Pole-dancing is a henparty activity we cannot recommend highly enough.

AFTERNOON ACTIVITIES – OUT OF THE ORDINARY

Cocktail-making
Some brides want an afternoon activity but also want to ensure that it will kick-start the party early in the day. An excellent way to combine the two is to have a cocktail-making lesson. You can choose between having a specially-trained bartender come to your home or holding a party in a venue organised by the cocktail expert. Keep an eye out for ads in off-licences or check online. Many bars and nightclubs offer cocktail-making classes, running these afternoon courses themselves. The barman will show you how it is done, with wrist-flicking and a lot of 'Oooh-ing' and 'Aaaaah-ing'. Learn how to make a real mojito and discover the proper ingredients for a Long Island iced tea. The ladies can have a go themselves and, more importantly, have a taste.

Painting a Nude
In Ireland you can now (tastefully of course) paint a nude male model for your henparty. Specialised art companies will bring paints and easels to any location around the country, with an artist to coach participants and a live male nude model. Guests at the henparty, once over the initial shock, can settle down to an afternoon of bona fide art, while the artist will give you guidance on colour, method and shading. Suitable for everybody from novices all the way to seasoned artists, this class is enjoyable, educational – and a great laugh.

Recording a Song

For the Mariah Carey wannabes amongst you, recording your own single is a truly rewarding way to spend the afternoon of the henparty. Many recording studios around the country are now offering this service to henparties and are happy to let you and your friends belt one out and record a CD as a keepsake of the day. The Internet is the best place to find these studios. While these afternoons are better for those with a note in their heads, hitting the odd 'off note' makes for plenty of laughs too. A trip to a recording studios may be slightly more expensive than the mainstream afternoon activities but it's an experience you probably will never have again, so go for it!

Having Your Palm Read

Clairvoyants can be found on most supermarket notice boards, in the newspapers and simply through word of mouth. This henparty activity is one with an edgy difference and not for the faint-hearted. Some ladies can't handle the stress of having their fortune told, so bear this is mind when booking. There's nothing like ladies hearing they will end up living alone with their cat to pour cold water on a night out. Most clairvoyants are happy to take henparty groups and will travel to your location. The bigger the group, the longer the whole afternoon takes, so this activity is not suited to groups larger than eight or ten people. This activity is becoming increasingly popular for henparties and gives guests something to talk about long into the night.

AFTERNOON ACTIVITIES – FLASHY

Chartering a Yacht
Push the boat out and show them how it is really done. Charter a yacht for your henparty and have an afternoon activity with serious style. Yacht charter companies are located in all the major sailing ports around the coast. To charter a yacht for the day is not cheap but if you are looking to blow the budget, it is an excellent choice. The accompanying skipper and deck hand will take care of sailing the vessel and making sure it stays afloat, while you and your henparty enjoy the life on the ocean wave. Champagne, nibbles and some tunes should set the mood. Most of these yachts are like small apartments below deck, so take advantage of the space and pack a really nice lunch or have someone make it for you. The word 'posh' was originally a maritime term, so show the ladies how a posh henparty rolls.

Helicopter Ride
More suited to a smaller henparty because of the space constraints, a helicopter ride is as flashy as an afternoon activity can get. Be the envy of all the girls at the tennis club as you soar over them into the blue. There is nothing quite so exciting as rising rapidly from ground zero to a sudden, breath-taking hundred-foot altitude in a matter of seconds. This thrill alone makes it worth the money spent. Then taking off across the town or country to see familiar sights from a bird's-eye view is unforgettable. Make sure everyone takes photos while in the air, as a helicopter ride will have them talking for years. There are

companies in every large city that will be happy to take your henparty out for the afternoon. Find them online or through the airports.

Skiing

Another activity with a touch of bling is an afternoon on the snow. There are now several Irish ski slopes both north and south of the border for you and your henparty to enjoy. Suitable for beginners and experienced skiers alike, an afternoon on the slopes is not only a great keep-fit exercise, it is a stylish and unusual way to have a henparty. Learn the basics of 'snow plough' and how to make it to the bottom without falling over. And of course no skiing outing would be complete without the après-ski – have some mulled wine in flasks in the car for the perfect end to the afternoon.

Golf

This is a wonderfully relaxing way for a henparty to spend an afternoon. A trip around the golf course is perfect for a small group and adds a touch of elegance to your event, at the same time being a lot of fun. Better suited to smaller and more intimate henparties, an afternoon on the links on a crisp day can be a refreshing alternative to a strenuous activity or something on the water. Some G&Ts and a few sandwiches back at the clubhouse bar afterwards will guarantee that it is a henparty to remember.

A word of warning for anyone planning an activity for a henparty: don't ever book a climbing wall. For my sister's henparty last year, her best friend was the maid of honour and organised the weekend. We were told to bring runners and comfortable clothing. I thought we were going horse-riding, which wouldn't have been so bad. I am not a small girl and was psychologically scarred by the harness I had to wear and the humiliation of trying to cling on to those little mounds on the wall and not fall off. I did, in fact I came off every time.

There were lots of really fit guys watching us as we were all wearing T-shirts with pictures of the bride on them and stood out as a henparty. I have never been so embarrassed in my life, especially as I didn't know loads of the other guests as they were my sister's friends from work. I ended up drinking too much at the meal to cover my embarrassment and made an ever bigger fool of myself. Never again.

Maggie

My best friend organised a pole dancing class for my henparty and I would recommend it as great fun for the night. It wasn't as hard to do as I thought it would be and we all laughed loads. My mum was on the henparty, so she became the official photographer and got some great pictures. The fun part was that we could let our hair down and kick up our heels – literally – but since it was a private class, there were no nosy onlookers or boozy guys to jeer at us. We just had a laugh.

Lorna

6

Dinner and Dressing Up

Dinner is the core element of the modern henparty; your meal is essentially the focal point of the day. For those who couldn't make it to the afternoon activity, or for those who are pregnant and won't be hitting the pubs, the meal is that special time when the Hen has all her girls around her. The glad rags are dusted off, the willy straws are passed around and the Hen sits in the centre or at the top of the table and laps up all the attention. The henparty meal is a must and it is here the 'Awww' moments are experienced, funny stories are recounted and the memories from the henparty are created. So for any maid of honour or Hen planning a henparty, take note: the meal is as important to the henparty as the marriage rite is to the wedding.

FINDING A HEN-FRIENDLY RESTAURANT

The biggest challenge in finding a restaurant is identifying one that will be happy to accommodate a henparty. Many restaurants simply don't want henparties, others turn a blind eye, while the remainder welcome them with open arms. When you are organising the henparty meal there are a few ways to approach the booking but to our mind the best approach is to keep it honest and simple.

For example: 'Hello, we are arriving in Galway for a henparty in February and wondering could we make a booking for twenty please?' Where a restaurant is henparty-friendly, they will take the booking and it is as simple as that. Alternatively, they might at this point thank you politely for your enquiry but explain that they don't cater for henparties. On the positive side, they will often recommend a great alternative eatery.

While we advocate honesty, there are limits. 'Hello, we are arriving in Galway for a henparty in February and would like to make a booking for twenty women dressed as Bollywood harem workers and a blow-up man who would also like his own chair.' There is coming clean and there is coming clean. Describing the devilment you have planned for the meal down to the colour of the stripper's undies is just not necessary. If you are going to play it safe and ask a restaurant outright, keep it simple.

Many ladies choose to omit some of the details. 'Hello, we are looking to book a table in February for about twenty people, please.' However the problem with not telling the truth is when the gang arrives wearing cowboy hats, feather boas and T-shirts with the Hen on the front, the restaurant may have a serious problem with it. Many high-end restaurants simply will not cater for henparties. Or where a restaurant has a family reputation and a henparty turns up with phallus-shaped straws, the likelihood is that the henparty will either be asked to leave or asked to remove all the paraphernalia.

Keeping it honest and simple will save you time in the

end, as you will find that there are plenty of restaurants out there that are really pleased with henparty trade. So take some time to find one and come clean. Rather than putting a dampener on the night or risking complaints from other guests, think ahead and find a restaurant that will be happy to let the girls wear their gear and even encourage the festivities. Risking any kind of complications on the night just isn't worth it.

PROCEEDINGS AT THE MEAL

At a typical henparty, everyone dresses up in their most glamorous attire and meets at the restaurant. Normally nobody is wearing henparty gear at this point, except where T-shirts have been printed and handed out in advance.

The Hen will be allowed to choose where she sits, or the maid of honour may have a seating plan. When setting out a seating plan, think it through. Putting two new mothers with their tales of epidurals next to two younger cousins with a penchant for Tequila is not a good idea. If you don't know the ladies well, try to get acquainted through other friends and be compassionate when seating guests together. The henparty meal can last for anything up to three hours and sets the tone for the night ahead. When people with things in common are seated next to each other, they are more likely to bond. Bonding at the henparty meal means only one thing… guaranteed group dancing later on in the night.

The meal begins and several bottles of wine usually kick-start proceedings. The ladies begin to chat and everyone starts to get in the spirit of things. For the maid of honour, it is fun either at the start or half-way through the meal to say a few words about the bride. She could also put a tiara on the bride's head, produce something funny or gorgeous for her to wear or tell a story about her. It just reminds everyone why they are there and, again, puts all the attention on the Hen.

Once the meal is over and the bill arrives, it is customary for the guests to split the bill. The Hen never pays. Everyone else chips in for the Hen. False protests of, 'Ah no, guys, I'll pay for myself,' are vainly put forward but tradition dictates that the Hen doesn't put her hand in her pocket.

WHAT NOT TO DO AT THE MEAL

There are a few points that should be taken on board when planning the meal. Firstly, strippers. Strippers and kissograms are great fun and at the right henparty, can be the best laugh of the night. They simply aren't suited to every situation, however, and it is important to know when they are not appropriate. If you are thinking of asking a stripper to the restaurant, you must always check with the restaurant first. Other patrons may find a stripper very offensive, particularly if there are children present. Even kissograms may be too much for some restaurants that would prefer to keep the tone of the henparty down slightly. Always check in advance.

It is also important to be sure that the Hen herself is going to be comfortable with a stripper. For the shy and quiet Hen who hasn't had too many boyfriends and is easily shocked, a stripper is not a good idea, no matter how funny you think the rest of the group will find it. Rubbing baby oil into Fabio's pecs may be your idea of heaven but it may not be the Hen's. Likewise if conservative mothers, or – worse still – mothers-in-law are at the meal, a male in a thong may not go down well at all.

Another no-no for the henparty meal is complaining. No bitching if the soup is cold or your steak is under-cooked. Once the dressing up and games begin, you're not allowed to complain about anything then, either. We won't elaborate on this point as everyone knows it's just not an option.

REASONS TO DRESS UP

When the meal is over and the coffees have been polished off, the fun part of the henparty meal begins: the dressing up. But the age-old henparty question remains – why in God's name would fifteen grown women want to dress up?

The answer is: because they can and because they want to. When else can a grown woman don a tiara, wave a wand and fly with her fairy wings? When else can a grown woman dress like a giant Playboy bunny and venture out in public with the rest of the herd – into a society perfectly accepting of it? When else can a group of grown women wear hula skirts and wigs, or Pocahontas outfits – and not be rounded up for the funny farm? Women dress up on henparties, quite simply because they can. The thrill of cutting loose, of standing out, of doing something you usually wouldn't do in your daily life is the idea behind it – and all in celebration of the Hen.

There is also the thrill of dressing up for a henparty and the attention that goes with it. On a normal night out with the girls, the men in the pub aren't liable to give you the once-over when you walk through the door. But if the whole groups is dressed like Naughty Schoolgirls, they most certainly will. It's all about the bravado, the craic, the licence to let loose, that feeling of being in a gang that is having so much fun. Dressing up for a henparty is like wearing a uniform that says to the rest of the world, 'We're out for our girl and we're having fun.' While a psychologist would surely find the whole thing 'fascinating', all we mere mortals have to know is that on a henparty, it is completely acceptable to wear boppers on your head and at the same time have an earnest conversation with another guest about the prevailing economic crisis.

And let's be honest ladies, there is another advantage to dressing up for henparties: if one of the ladies goes missing it won't be a hard job to find her. 'Yes, Garda, she was wearing white knee-high platform boots, a sparkly mini skirt and a pink wig down to her navel. Oh, and she has a "Kiss me – I'm cute" badge on her left false breast'…

REASONS NOT TO DRESS UP
There are many reasons women don't dress up for their henparties. This choice is perfectly fine too. Some ladies, for one reason or another, just aren't as excited about dressing up as others. This is completely normal and should be accepted by all on the henparty. If the Hen says, 'No,' then it probably isn't the best idea to plan

full-length nun outfits as a surprise. If the Hen has her reasons for not dressing up, those around her should respect them and not force anything on her. After all, it's her big night and whatever her reasons are, they are valid. A more subtle method of identifying the bride can usually be found, a simple black T-shirt with 'The Hen' elegantly printed on it being one.

Fear of embarrassment is another common reason for a henparty going 'gear-less'. For many women this fear is simply too great to overcome and as a result they will opt to have a low-key affair in terms of dressing up. They would prefer to go out for their henparty and blend into the background, attracting as little attention as possible. Strippers, straws and slippery nipples would be humiliating beyond belief to them, so these henparties remain, in terms of dressing up, sedate affairs.

Of all the excuses brides give for not dressing up, the 'It won't go with my outfit' brigade have the best. There is a breed of lady in our midst who endeavours to look absolutely perfect at all times. Hair highlighted, nails gelled, top lip waxed and eyebrows arched to perfection. For these ladies, dressing up for her henparty is simply not an option, since, realistically, what sort of outfit could a feather boa genuinely complement? To wear fluffy love cuffs with a Donna Karan fishbone dress would not only cheapen the dress, it would detract from the accessories. 'Hen' sashes are never going to go with a Max Mara coat.

Whatever the reason a Hen has given for not wishing to dress up, or have the whole party dressed up, it is important to respect her wishes. Having one or two small props in your handbag to test the waters can be worth considering to mark the night in some small way.

DRESSING UP IDEAS
Lots and lots of themes are available for a henparty, some more over the top than others. When selecting what the group will wear, think it through. If you have a mixed age group, a pimps and prostitutes theme will probably not work so well. Likewise, if several of the group happen to be larger ladies, having a hot pants theme may upset a few of them. Ultimately everyone will wear what they are told but it is in the best interests of the night and the mood of the group to make sure that people are semi-comfortable if they are asked to dress up.

The Neutral Henparty
When in doubt, keep it safe. A pair of discreet devil horns or bunny-rabbit ears are often enough for a henparty. Sometimes just giving everyone a henparty fan or a whistle to wear around their necks can do the trick. A henparty badge is another option, with a headpiece or on its own. These props don't interfere with what people are wearing, they are cheap to buy and won't take up much space on the way to the location. They are ideal for a quiet henparty, a mixed age group or for a Hen who doesn't care what people wear. Refreshingly simple.

Playboy Bunnies
This timeless classic is still popular at many henparties. Ask guests to dress in black, the sexier the better. You can then pass around the bunny sets, which include ears,

a playboy collar and of course the bunny tail. This is an extremely effective theme, as the black and white is very striking. Fifteen henparty Playboy bunnies walking on to the floor of the nightclub can stop the locals dead in their tracks.

Saucy Devils

Other popular choices for today's henparties are saucy devils outfits. Again ask all the guests to dress in black and on the night pass out the devil's horns. Fire-engine-red boas set the outfit off to a tee. Complete saucy devil sets are available in many stores and include horns, a tail and a sceptre. Like the Playboy bunny theme, this is extremely effective and on occasions when there are several henparties in a bar or nightclub, the Saucy Devils will be visible every time.

Naughty Nuns

Who would have guessed that dressing up as a nun could be so much fun? Simply ask all the guests, once again, to dress in black: little black dresses are ideal for this particular theme. Pass out the nuns' headdresses and bless me father for I have sinned…The nuns' theme is only just catching on, so chances are you will have the only gear of this kind in town. It's also relatively inexpensive and is suitable for women of all age groups and sizes.

Hawaiian Hula

Aloha. Grass skirts and garlands of flowers are all that are needed for a Hawaiian-themed henparty. Many henparties opt for this theme if there are dance classes for the afternoon activity. This way, there is a theme to the whole day. It is easy, cheap and guaranteed to get your henparty attention. For a truly Hawaiian hula henparty, book a cocktail class and learn to make Hawaiian blue or volcano cocktails.

Pimps and Prostitutes

A fairly self-explanatory theme for dressing up, this is one that works well when there is a big group at the henparty. Two 'prostitutes' and two 'pimps' in a pub might look decidedly odd. For the pimps, gold chains, velvet clothes, big hats and fly-guy glasses are the order of the day. For the prostitutes, it's black eyeliner, short skirts and fishnet stockings. Your imagination is all that stops you with this one.

Cowgirls

The cowgirl theme is always a big hit with the ladies on a henparty, as it doesn't interfere with wearing their own outfit underneath. Cowboy hats come in a variety of neon colours and shapes. Teamed with a custom-printed T-shirt, they can make a fun theme for a henparty. Don't forget to bring along a nice Stetson for your blow-up bloke as well.

Naughty Schoolgirls

One of our favourites, the naughty schoolgirl theme will guarantee attention from the gentlemen all night. It's a relatively inexpensive and easy-to-organise theme for a henparty. All you need is a shirt, a tie, a short skirt and knee-high socks. Add big hair and heavy make-up and you've got the look. Most ladies can borrow their dads'jumpers and ties and throw a mini skirt with them. Perfect.

Sex and the City

There are two interpretations of the *Sex and the City* theme and both are good fun for a henparty. Basically, if glam is the order of the day, saying the henparty theme is *SATC* gives the ladies licence to go mad. Little black dresses, fabulous accessories, stunning hairdos and killer heels – all make a great theme for the fashion conscious, or for a henparty with a bit of class. The other version is to try and actually dress like one of the four characters from the show. A little more challenging but anything is possible with some good wigs and a little imagination.

1970s Theme

Bell bottoms, flower-power beads, long wigs and peace logos are all the elements needed for a 1970s henparty. Ask the guests to dig through their own or their mothers' wardrobes and bring back the 1970s! Think glam rock, fabulous groupies or ABBA hot pants. Think platform shoes, Mary Quant eyeliner, David Bowie hairdos and Elton John specs! This theme is great for a small gang, or in a small town or village, as the party will really stand out.

Pink Ladies

For this theme, pink is the order of the night. Ladies wear wigs and pink jackets to match, proving that the cult hit *Grease* is still alive and well in Ireland, with many henparties reliving the film. The jackets and wigs are available in most good novelty stores and although it is a little more expensive than the other themes, this one will certainly make your henparty stand out.

Bollywood Babes
With the continued success and higher profile of Bollywood on this side of the world, the Bollywood theme is a hit for henparties in Ireland. A sari is relatively easy to find or make these days and with your own outfit underneath for the nightclub, it can be a great focus for the evening. Coupled with a Bollywood dance class, this theme is great fun, feminine and easy to achieve. Henna makes the look even more authentic.

Flappers
Flapper outfits look great, suit any shape or age and are incredibly feminine. There is a multitude of flapper outfits available in fancy dress shops and novelty shops and the choice is both enormous and varied. These are great outfits for a daring henparty and look extremely effective on the dance floor and in the pub.

Wigs
Not every henparty has a full-blown theme and there are many alternatives to fifteen bunnies or fifteen devils. Some brides or maids of honour simply choose wigs for the guests to wear. Blonde, red, curly, long, short – the possibilities are endless. They will mark the group as a henparty but without the cumbersome gear that goes with a full-blown theme.

T-shirts

As with wigs, many ladies who attend henparties don't choose to wear the traditional henparty paraphernalia but still want to be recognisable as a group. T-shirts are perfect for achieving this. Custom-printed T-shirts are hugely popular on henparties and most vendors will provide flattering lady-fit styles: 'Mary's Henparty, Winstown, 2009' or 'I Am on Claire's Henparty' or 'Henparty on Tour'. Many vendors will print pictures on T-shirts and these can be hilarious, such as a photo of the bride as a child, making her Holy Communion. Or why not put a picture of the groom-to-be on a T-shirt and make the bride wear it. T-shirts also make a lovely keepsake from the henparty.

> I had my henparty last summer and my friend told us all to wear sexy black outfits to the meal. I wasn't sure what to expect and I know some of the other girls were a bit nervous about what she had planned. We came down to dinner and first had a drink in the bar and we were all in our black outfits. Next thing Sally comes running in wearing a nun's veil and habit and a giant cross. It was the funniest thing I have ever seen. I nearly died laughing and she passed out a veil to everyone there. We all had to pick a 'saucy sister's' name and wear name badges with them for the night.
>
> *Orla*

My friend didn't want to dress up for her henparty, so I just got a T-shirt printed for her with her name on it and the date of the henparty. She's shy enough and made it clear from the start she wasn't interested in any of that fancy gear. One of the other bridesmaids thought we should dress her up anyway but I'm glad we didn't, because she really didn't want to. We all had a brilliant time in the end anyway, so it turned out best for everybody to respect her feelings.

Magda

7

HENPARTY GAMES

Henparty games, just like the meal and dressing up, are a key element to any successful henparty. They are what makes the night different from any other night out with the girls and they can make the Hen feel very special, as well as generating big laughs. They are usually played with the coffee after the meal and can be as tame or as wild as you make them. Essentially they are more about making a fuss of the Hen than anything. After all, if this book has taught you nothing else, it should at this stage have taught you that it is always all about the Hen.

What exactly are henparty games? Basically, they are traditional games such as 'Mr and Mrs' and 'Either/Or', and many other games can be used with a little bit of a 'Hen' slant put on them. We will explain them in more detail later in the chapter.

Henparty games are a means of lavishing attention on the Hen, often embarrassing her, always making her laugh, and entertaining those around the table. They make the Hen stand out and show the effort and trouble that you, her friends, have gone to on this very special night. Some games involve the Hen answering questions; others involve members of the group telling stories, while others still can involve small props or even heavy-duty equipment. Knowing the Hen and knowing her humiliation limits are important when choosing henparty games.

TO HAVE OR NOT TO HAVE HENPARTY GAMES
There are many reasons to have henparty games, the first and most important being that they are great fun! Picture the scene; twenty women all watching the Hen decide whether her husband-to-be correctly guessed her bra size. It can only mean a lot of laughs. Everyone gets into the spirit of the night, there is a huge fuss made of the Hen, and the outing is marked as something different from any other night out with friends.

Playing party games with friends (not to mention the idea of dressing up to do so) is not something most of us do any longer, so to play with such props and answer a lot of silly questions for the pure entertainment of it is simply a lot of fun. And no one is going to judge us for it.

Hen games can also be a clever way of dressing up a very shy Hen without simply covering her in sashes, bunny ears and boas. Playing one of the quizzes (see them listed later in this chapter) creates a situation where, if the Hen answers incorrectly, she has to put on a piece of paraphernalia – an L-plate for example. It is an easy way to mark the Hen without making her uncomfortable and she can take the gear off afterwards.

There are situations where games will not be appropriate. If the Hen is mature and is perhaps getting married for the second time, shaming her by playing games that tell stories of ex-boyfriends and drunken college nights is clearly not going to be acceptable. Similarly, asking a very conservative group of girls to build the best willy possible with playdough may lead to upset and distress. Many restaurants are not suitable for this kind of behaviour and whether you are having a classy meal or a flashy henparty, the reality may be that henparty games won't be possible.

WHAT NOT TO DO FOR HENPARTY GAMES

While everyone loves humiliating the Hen and having a great laugh at her expense, boundaries must be drawn. Think of the bride's personality when you are planning henparty games. We all laugh at the squirming Hen dodging questions about ex-boyfriends, but be careful never to go too close to the mark. A Hen may be sensitive about her past, and while two or three at the table may know her darkest, most shameful secrets, she may not appreciate everyone else knowing them as well: especially if mothers, mothers-in-law to be and older relatives are present. The Hen may not thank you for sharing the story of that college night she shinned up a lamp post in her underwear, only to remain there until the fire brigade was called.

Also be conscious of vulgarity levels at this stage of the night, paying special attention to the other guests at the henparty. The bridesmaids may find it hilarious blowing up an inflatable man and covering him in whipped cream. The Hen's mother may not find it as hilarious. If there are older ladies on the henparty or younger relatives, be mindful of having fun but keeping it out of the gutter.

HENPARTY GAMES
There are lots of henparty games out there to choose from. Here are some of our favourites:

Mr and Mrs
An oldie but a goodie. Simply take the questions below and ask the groom to answer them before the henparty. On the night ask the Hen to answer the same set of questions. Her answers must match the groom's, or else she must do a forfeit. This can be either to take a swig from her drink or to perform a dare if you have a pack of dare cards handy. Let the Hen see how well she really knows her man!

- What is *his* confirmation name?
- How often does *he* change his socks?
- What shirt collar size does *he* wear?
- What is *his* favourite movie?
- What is *her* worst habit (according to *him*)?
- Which of them does the most cooking at home?
- Which female movie/TV star does *he* fancy?
- What is *his* favourite cocktail?
- In which position does *he* play…on the field?
- What was the name of *his* favourite childhood pet?

- Which of *his* relatives does *she* like least?
- Which of *her* relatives does *he* like least?
- What is *her* favourite cocktail?
- What is the name of *her* first boyfriend?
- How old was *he* when he first kissed a girl?
- What is *her* bra size? (no peeking)
- What is *his* favourite book?
- Which movie/TV star does *he* think *he* is most like?
- What is *his* favourite piece of *her* lingerie?
- Which of them will be the more hungover after the wedding?

Either/Or

Another henparty classic, this game once again shows how well the Hen knows her husband and is guaranteed to generate uproar around the table. As before, take the choices below and before the henparty, ask the groom to choose which he prefers. On the night, the Hen must say what she thinks the groom answered. If she is wrong she must do a forfeit: as before, this can be a swig of her drink or a dare:

- Blonde or brunette
- Waxed or shaved
- Melons or fried eggs
- Home or abroad
- Trashy or classy
- Larsson or Hartson
- Football or rugby
- McDonald's or Burger King

- Chinese or curry
- Glasgow or Edinburgh
- Town or country
- Lager or heavy
- Port or whiskey
- Angelina or Jessica (Alba)
- Bum or tits
- Sun or ski
- Tea or coffee
- Boxers or briefs
- Spit roast or Yorkshire pudding
- Lap dance or breakdance
- Ballet or opera
- Posh or Becks
- Sharapova or Kournikova
- Timberland or Timberlake
- Normandy or Britney
- Connery or Connolly
- Monopoly or Cluedo
- PlayStation or Xbox
- Trainers or loafers
- Rooney or Lampard
- Twosome or threesome
- Deeley or Daly (Kat or Tess)
- Batman or Spiderman
- Casino or horse racing
- Dungeons and Dragons or He-Man
- Cats or dogs
- Snickers or Mars
- Blow-jobs or hand-jobs
- Nike or Adidas

- Space Hopper or Lo-Lo Ball
- Phil Collins or Mick Hucknall
- Tony Blackburn or Jimmy Saville
- Starter or dessert
- GQ or FHM
- Ferrari or Maserati
- Hungry Hippos or Buckaroo
- J-Lo or Beyoncé
- Rough or smooth
- *Star Trek* or *Star Wars*
- Ant or Dec

The Bubblegum Game

This game is not for the faint-hearted but it generates a lot of laughter and is one of the funniest henparty games there is. It's also very simple to do. Simply write a list of questions about the groom and get him to answer them before the henparty. On the night, make the Hen stand up and ask her to answer each question. For every question she gets wrong she must put a piece of bubblegum in her mouth. For obvious reasons the more questions and the harder they are the funnier the game. Just be careful she doesn't choke as it would put an awful dampener on the party...

Truth or Dare

Truth or dare can be the funniest game of the night. Everyone at the table gets to ask the Hen a really embarrassing question. If she won't answer she must perform one of the dares below: if she won't do the dare, she must have a shot of booze:

- Ask a stranger to buy you a drink.
- Ask a stranger for his autograph.
- Ask a guy for change for the condom machine.
- Shout out loud that you are not wearing any underwear.
- Ask a man in uniform for a kiss.
- Get the phone number of a man whose name begins with a particular letter.
- Do a pre-designed dance every time someone shouts out a certain song title to you (for example, *Riverdance* or 'YMCA').
- Find and kiss two brothers/cousins.
- Remove an item of underwear without leaving the room.

The Five Decades of Underwear Game
Not so much of an activity game for the Hen, this game instead makes a statement about married life to come. Wrap five pairs of knickers and pass to the Hen to be unwrapped one by one:

- For the first, tell her it represents the honeymoon period and put a lacy thong inside.
- For the second, tell her it represents the second decade of marriage, or the 'getting comfy period' and put a pair of sexyish briefs inside.
- For the third, wrap a pair of boy shorts and tell her they represent the third decade of marriage, or 'the kids all over the gaff' era.

- For the fourth, wrap a frumpy pair of sensible knickers and tell her it represents the fourth decade, or 'after the kids'.
- For the fifth and final package, tell her it represents the fifth and final decade of marriage – when she just won't care any more. Wrap the biggest ugliest granny pants you can find.

Pin the Body Part on the Hunk

This game is a bit like 'Pin the Tail on the Donkey' but adapted for henparties. Take a poster of a very attractive male, preferably with his top off. Even better, try and get a photograph of the groom and blow it up. Either draw body parts, or cut them out of a magazine and attach blue-tack to the back. Blindfold the Hen. Telling her what body part she is holding and ask her to pin it on the man. For each incorrect 'placing' the Hen must perform a forfeit. As before, this could be to take a swig of a drink, or having to perform a dare. Everyone in the group can have a go and while we would not in a million years advocate vulgarity, clearly the more imagination used when picking the body parts the better.

Snog the Sex-God

A hilarious version of 'Pin the Body Part on the Hunk'. This time, instead of attaching body parts to the blown-up picture, ask the Hen to on put bright red lipstick. Blindfold her and ask her to kiss the hunk on the lips. If she misses she has to do a forfeit.

Master Sculptor
This is a naughty make-and-do game for the whole group at the meal. Simply take playdough and pass a piece to everyone at the table. The aim of the game is to build the best willy in sixty seconds. The Hen gets to choose the winner (and of course she can choose her own if she deems it to be the best). The winner gets a small prize, such as a drink from the bar or a scratch card.

True or False
The True or False game is a henparty activity that takes a little time and should only be proposed where the organiser knows that the Hen will feel comfortable being publicly humiliated. It is not for a fragile or sensitive Hen. The game also needs to be organised by someone who knows the Hen well, or put another way, has serious dirt on her!

1. Write out ten or more short, really embarrassing stories about the bride. Under each write 'True or False?' For example, if you know the Hen once kissed a lecturer from college that could be one of your stories.
2. Print a copy for each guest at the henparty and title the sheet 'True or False?'
3. During or after the henparty meal, pass around the sheets and ask the guests to read through them and tick off which stories are true and which are false. Then the maid of honour gets up and reads out the correct answers. The killer, of course, is that all the stories will be true.

This game will work only if the stories are really embarrassing. Be mindful: this is not a game to play where mothers or mothers-in-law are present, or where the Hen may not see the funny side of her secrets being revealed. Otherwise it is an extremely funny henparty game.

The Note Game
This is a great henparty game as it gives everyone a chance to tell a story and get involved. Simply hand everyone a small piece of paper and ask them to write *one* line that refers to a memory they have of the Hen. Put all the pieces of paper in a cup and ask the Hen to pick them out, one by one. She must read out the line, tell the group who wrote the line and what the story refers to. If the Hen is too shy to tell the story or simply doesn't remember it she must perform a forfeit, either take a swig of her drink or do a dare. For this game, the more embarrassing the stories the better.

Henparty Survival Kit
Like 'Five Decades of Marital Underwear', this game is really a show-and-tell rather than a game that requires the Hen to get involved. Simply decorate an old shoebox or find a nice container and fill it with the items you think the Hen will need to get through the henparty successfully. These could include:

- Paracetamol
- A list of 'emergency' phone numbers in case she gets lost

- A miniature bottle of brandy for her nerves
- A picture of the groom to remind her why she is there
- Eye makeup remover wipes (in case she is too tired going to bed)

And more. The better you know the Hen, the more you can put in the box. This game can also be modified and called 'Marriage Survival Kit', with baby name books, batteries for the remote control and so on.

You're Marrying Him?

This is a henparty game that lasts for the whole night. Before the henparty ask the groom or his mother for the worst photo they can find of *him*. Really now, ladies, we mean *bad*. Blow it up and give it to the Hen on the night. For the rest of the night whenever someone shouts a particular code word ('minger' being a good one), the Hen must approach a stranger, tell them she is getting married and show them a picture of the man himself. Believe me, the henparty guests will nearly laugh themselves sick.

Dare Cards

Dare cards should be a staple at everyone's henparty. Already packaged and ready to go, they can be used at the meal, after the meal, at the pub, in the car – wherever. Dare cards come in a box of about thirty and range from, 'Ask a man in uniform for his number' to 'Kiss two brothers'. Everyone gets to pick one and you must do your dare! The creative among you could make your own dare cards and personalise them with pictures of the Hen.

> My husband-to-be guessed nearly every question wrong for the Mr and Mrs quiz. I was so embarrassed and started to wonder if he know me at all! The girls were in hysterics, of course, and gave me grief over it for the whole night. Honestly, if he had been there I would have killed him!
>
> *Noreen*

> The funniest henparty I was at was one where, when we were leaving a nice restaurant to find a pub, the Hen's sisters grabbed her and held her up against a wall. Out of nowhere someone produced a blow-up man and they handcuffed her to him for the night. Everywhere we went, lads were offering to buy 'him' drinks. Hysterical.
>
> *Susie*

8

PUBS AND CLUBS

Once the meal is finished, the games are over and the costumes are on, it's time to hit the pubs. The majority of henparties following the traditional model will, at this point, move on for drinks and dancing after the meal. Ideally, start somewhere quiet where everyone can get served quickly and sober chats can continue. After the first or second pub, the norm is to settle in one place for a few drinks before moving on to the nightclub.

When choosing a pub for the post-meal drinkies, don't be too concerned about where you go. If you know the town or city already and are familiar with the best venues, that is obviously an advantage. On the other hand, if you don't, remember that the pub itself is not what will determine whether or not you have a good night but rather how the group is getting on. This is where all your preparation efforts come to fruition: you've set a good tone for the party during the afternoon and the meal and now it's time for everybody to let the hair down.

If you have the inside track on a particularly great place for the girls, then you should absolutely use it. Perhaps you know of a rugby pub in town where the gentlemen will be only too delighted to welcome a henparty? Or perhaps someone has tipped you off about a wonderful bar that serves the most amazing cocktails. Any inside information about where to go should be availed of for this, the big event. But we stress that it's not the end of the world if you just take things as they come. We guarantee that by this stage, the Hen and her guests will be in such good form that they'll make any venue their own. Sometimes discovering little gems of locations in this way can be half the fun.

HENPARTIES, PUBS AND PROBLEMS
One of the biggest problems encountered by henparties is admission to pubs and night-time venues. In many of the larger towns in particular, you may find getting into pubs to be a challenge. Pub proprietors feel that henparty groups are trouble and that they lower the tone of the pub, so when the bouncers see a troupe wearing cowboy hats on the horizon, they will very often have the 'not tonight folks' line at the ready. Others may let the party in but insist that all the henparty gear is removed. It can throw a real dampener on the night for ladies to have spent time dressing up, only to be told to take all the fun gear off again. Our advice in situations like this is to make light of the situation and find another pub, because no amount of, 'Please Mr Bouncer, please, please, please,' is going to make these guys change their minds. The policy comes from the management.

To be more certain of avoiding a situation where the henparty will be refused at every second pub, try opting for a smaller town or somewhere you know that has a 'henparty-friendly' reputation. Many of the henparty hotspots from five years ago are just not keen on henparties any more, so make some enquiries before you go booking. Kilkenny was once henparty heaven but more recently it decided to shed its henparty reputation and is less than welcoming. Places like Waterford are still only too happy to take henparties and there are few, if any, problems getting into pubs and clubs.

The bottom line here is to do a little bit of research. Ask someone who has been in a place before, or if you are really stuck, why not ring a pub from the phone book and just ask outright whether the town is henparty-friendly. This will save you anxiety about being refused admission on the night itself.

Returning to an issue we already partially covered, it's worth double-checking ahead of time about whether or not another henparty has already booked into the same pub or club. In larger cities and towns this is nearly always going to be the case, so be prepared not to be the only henparty in the building. If you're concerned that the Hen is going to have a showdown with the rival Hen in the pub, plan ahead where possible. Otherwise, if you can see bunny ears or boas through the window, best try somewhere else.

Fun Things to Do in the Pub
There are many fun things that can be organised at the pub to keep the atmosphere fresh and to focus on the Hen. There is nothing worse than a Hen having all that attention lavished on her up to nine o'clock in the evening, only to have everyone start thinking exclusively

about themselves, neglecting the main point of the exercise...So keep the momentum going and use some of these nifty ideas to keep her happy:

If you arrive in a pub that has a DJ, get him to play a request for the Hen. Even better, ask him to play her favourite song and announce that she's getting married. This will give the Hen a huge thrill and turn all the attention back to her. The rest of the group should also get a thrill out of it.

It can also be the perfect moment to pull out the aforementioned pack of dare cards. These are small and fit in a handbag but when produced in the pub, can bring a dying henparty back to life or heighten the spirits of an already lively henparty. Dare cards are generally clean and don't involve anything too taxing. Dares along the lines of, 'Kiss the next man who comes through the door,' and, 'Tell a guy you're sure he's a big celebrity in disguise and ask him for his autograph,' are the norm. Most gentlemen are happy to oblige and some are delighted with the attention.

In terms of party paraphernalia, leaving one item for the Hen to put on in the pub can also be a good idea. This will once again focus the attention on her, while generating a laugh. Or why not wait until your arrival in the pub to hand out the Willy Straws? Again, this will keep the momentum of the night going.

Another small gesture that can make the Hen feel very special is booking into a VIP room. Many pubs these days have small separate VIP areas for private parties and functions: nothing too elaborate, but an area with bar service and some nice seating, slightly away from the 'great unwashed'. These VIP areas are generally free and are ideal for henparties. Find one in advance and book it. The pubs will often throw in a bottle of champagne as well, since it's in their interest to fill the space with cocktail-purchasing ladies.

THE NIGHTCLUB

And so to the final part of the evening: moving on to the nightclub. This is really where the moves are let loose and the girls all circle the Hen for some cheesy 1980s hits – 'Like a Prayer' being one of the top choices. The nightclub is where the shots are slammed, the requests are played and the tomfoolery of the night happens.

It's worth noting that many nightclubs will not welcome henparties with open arms. In larger cities, many will actually have a ban on them, while others, like pubs, will ask guests to remove all the henparty paraphernalia before they go inside. Luckily, in most decent-sized towns there is usually more than one nightclub, so find one in advance that will let you wear all your henparty gear and won't put any restrictions on your festivities.

Another advantage to a little pre-event research is that you'll probably find many nightclubs that love henparties and that will even offer incentives to bring them in. If you are visiting a town or city, it is well worth identifying such nightclubs in advance and contacting them. Many will offer half-price concessions to henparties, while others will even offer complimentary VIP areas and champagne. A handy tip is to call ahead and tell them you are coming.

Late bars are another option. Many late bars have the excellent combination of a good pub seating area and a dance floor. This way, those who aren't inclined to shake their booties can sit in comfort and continue chatting, while those who are up for it can let loose on the dance floor. The other advantage to a late bar is that admission is usually free, whereas a nightclub can be expensive, especially considering the few hours you are inside.

I thought it was so sweet at my henparty when we were in the nightclub at the end of the night. My friend had gone up to the DJ and he put my name in lights on the display board behind the decks and also mentioned that it was my henparty. I felt so special!

Emily

My friends and I took over the nightclub completely at my henparty. We were in a right dive and there weren't that many people there, so we had the whole dance floor to ourselves. We completely bullied the DJ and made him play everything we asked, which he did. It was like our own private club and it was brill.

Breda

9

THE GOLDEN HENPARTY

Don't let the young ones have all the fun. If you are getting married for the second time or are in your golden years, don't let anyone tell you that you shouldn't have a henparty. Second marriages and later marriages are commonplace these days. Luckily for us, society has finally realised that some women just aren't ready to get married in their twenties, while others may not have had the best luck first time around. More mature Hens should enjoy as much as any young woman being spoiled and celebrated on their last night of freedom.

Henparties celebrate women of all ages and status and there is a range of options available for your golden henparty. Push the boundaries if you feel like doing something really different: bungee jumping, quad biking, learning to jive. If the younger age group's preference for a razzmatazz henparty isn't for you, then there is plenty of scope for something more low-key or unusual. Whether it's your first, second or even third marriage, mark the occasion with your friends and family.

If camping or quad biking isn't your thing and you hung up your pole-dancing shoes years ago, choose something more laid-back that you and your friends will all enjoy. Think about your own tastes and if you are organising the henparty yourself – which most golden Hens do – book something accordingly. Here are a few examples of what may suit you and your guests:

DANCE CLASS
Ever wanted to learn how to salsa? Or maybe you often think about learning to swing. Dance class teachers are everywhere and nothing is easier than booking a dance class for your henparty. Enjoy a couple of hours of great laughs and sharp moves. A dance class spans the generations, so everyone at your henparty should enjoy the afternoon. Ask at your local dance studio for freelance teachers or keep an eye out in the papers.

GOURMET FOOD DAY
While some mature hens may feel they've done enough cooking to last a lifetime it's also possible to take an innovative approach to it, so that the mature Hen and friends can learn some new, specialised skills to enhance their kitchen savvy. A gourmet food day is a great idea for those who aren't interested in a sporty outing and want to have a civilised and fun day out. Most such events start early in the morning and the group observes the chef until lunchtime. Then they get to discuss the food and sample the culinary delights. For the afternoon, the Chef will once again show the group how it is done and some cookery schools will allow the group to try cooking for themselves. Dinner and wine are then served and once again your henparty gets to enjoy the

quality cuisine. Many of the top-level cookery schools are in period houses, with wonderful gardens to walk in, which makes a lovely day out. Research your ideal demo day online, or you can always ask in local restaurants whether they know of anywhere they can recommend as a venue. Gourmet food days are a lovely golden henparty outing – fun, relaxing and enough to make your button pop.

AFTERNOON TEA

There is a lot to be said for an old-fashioned silver-service afternoon tea at a five-star hotel. Or even in one of the large old houses of the former gentry, which frequently feature tea in their elegant drawing rooms. Dainty petit-fours, exquisite sandwiches and melt-in-the-mouth cake are served on fine china in beautiful, relaxing surroundings. Enjoy the pampering as you are waited on hand and foot for your henparty. Afterwards, take a stroll by the old lily-pond. On your return, you can always snuggle into an easy chair by a roaring fire in the hotel bar for a hot toddy! Since it's definitely something you wouldn't do every day, afternoon tea is a very impressive ritual when it is done properly and will lend a unique touch to the occasion. For the discerning lady, the afternoon tea outing is a must.

SPA DAY

One of the nice things about a pampering yourself is that there's definitely no age limit involved! Younger ladies need not be the only ones to enjoy the benefits of the luxury spas so prevalent across the country. A day of treatments is an excellent idea for a golden henparty and always goes down a storm with guests. Book a nice spa afternoon for yourself and the ladies, then relax and indulge yourself in preparation for your big day. Let an attractive young Swedish god ease the knots from your back and help you forget your woes – or why not splash out and book into a resort spa for the whole weekend. This will be cost-effective in terms of the many packages on offer for just such events – again, check online for the possibilities. It will also generate some genuine personal relaxation and provide you with a wonderful, chilled-out base from which to finalise preparations for the wedding itself. Enjoy dinner and drinks on top of the pampering. After all, you deserve it.

DAY ON THE GOLF COURSE
For golfing ladies, a day on the golf course followed by dinner in the clubhouse is a perfect idea for a golden henparty. Enjoy a few holes, take in the fresh air and enjoy the chats on the green. Have a couple of G&Ts after dinner and make a real outing of it. For a break from your usual haunt, why not book into a golf resort further afield. Most decent golf clubs have their own self-catering cottages, which can be really fun, and golf resort hotels often offer accommodation packages with golfing and dinner included. That way, you can stay overnight and enjoy some quality time away.

ART CLASS
For ladies who don't fancy the formality of the golf course or the stuffiness of the spa, a day-long painting

workshop might just fit the bill. There are one-day courses run all over the country and a local art dealer or gallery should be able to point you in the right direction. These courses offer light refreshments or lunch and most will cater for beginners, experienced painters and those in-between. Such courses are often located in beautiful country locations, such as artists' retreats, or galleries by the sea. This makes for a very relaxing day and provides something interesting for all ages in the group.

GOLDEN HEN NIGHTS

Golden hens may be busy career women and/or mothers who would prefer quality, not quantity, when it comes to committing time to a henparty. Some ladies don't want an all-day affair and would prefer to attend only an evening outing. This is perfectly acceptable too. Again, ladies, it is all down to taste.

Night-time henparties conjure up images of wild young women rampaging around pubs in costume. But of course henparties don't have to be all about alcohol, pinching bottoms and hitting the dance floor! For the more mature woman, there is nothing nicer than a classy night out with her family and friends. The golden henparty provides plenty of options. Here are a few examples:

Theatre and Dinner

The classic evening out for forty-somethings and more would probably be dinner followed by a trip to the theatre. Many theatres have deals with local restaurants where early bird menus and tickets can be bought at very reasonable prices. Ring the local theatre and ask them to send you a programme of upcoming shows. Or push the boat out and travel to a larger city where you can take in a show, have dinner and stay overnight in one of the excellent hotels.

Cinema Evening

Since a mature Hen's schedule is often taken up with kids, family chores, business meetings or all of the above, many of her friends may well appreciate the simple, fun option of a night at the movies. It's the perfect excuse for an escape that doesn't take up too much time or break the bank: popcorn, a film, a nice bite to eat beforehand. How many of us go to the cinema en masse any more? Wouldn't it be a lovely outing for your golden henparty? The cinema should definitely be considered for a nice, quiet, close-to-home henparty.

Dinner at Home

You would be surprised how overlooked this option is for a golden henparty. A 'girls' night in' evening at home with some good food, a few bottles of wine and some games can be the perfect option for your henparty. You can pull out all the stops and whip up some gourmet dishes to impress your friends or, better still, spoil yourself and hire a caterer. No-one will tell! For mortgage-bound ladies, this is the perfect option and you could even consider making it a 'pot luck' evening, where each guest brings a dish. This way the other women can show off a bit too and the costs are comfortably shared. Guests may feel more at ease at your house, making for guaranteed laughs at the recounting of old stories, no holds barred! Sometimes, ladies, less is more, so consider dinner at your home or at a friend's home for your big night.

City Break
While not strictly a night-time event, a city break is a memorable way to celebrate your henparty, perfect for a small group made up of sisters and daughters. Dust off those glad rags and take in some shows. Visit the local sights and spoil yourself in the shops. This is the ultimate girlie weekend and what better way to celebrate your send-off? You may even want to look for part of your wedding outfit on the trip; shoes, bags or hair accessories. Having the girls in tow will make this easy and a lot more fun. How about doing a 'shoe hunt', where the whole group has to chip in to purchase the sexiest pair of shoes ever for the bride's going-away outfit? You can then review the purchase over a 'late lunch' break at one of the excellent eateries found in any Irish city these days, or opt for a lovely afternoon tea in one of the older hotels before heading home. Pricewise this may be a more expensive option than some of the others we suggested, but it is one that will leave all concerned with some precious memories.

GOLDEN HENPARTY GAMES
Fun is fun and it goes without saying that there is nobody racier and wilder at the henparty games than a bunch of ladies with a few years of experience in the sack behind them! If you are having your henparty at home, or have some time at the restaurant or golf club, why not lift the

mood and add some craic to the proceedings. Here are some of the best:

Maiden Names

Write down all the maiden names of the guests coming to the henparty and make a copy of the list for each person. During dinner, pass the lists to everybody and ask them to match the guests to their maiden name. The winner is the person who has the most correct answers and gets a small prize.

Charades

Have a game of charades after dinner and continue the fun. There are many clues available online for those who don't have the time to pick some themselves. Or why not throw a different slant on the game and pick a theme – for example old movies – and have all the clues centred on that. Split the henparty guests into two teams and let each person take turns miming the charade within an agreed time-frame. The winning team is the team that answers the most correct mimes. Charades never go out of fashion and never fail to make people laugh.

Anagrams

As guests arrive at the party, give them a badge to wear with an anagram written on it. Badges are easy to make, just a rectangle of card with a safety pin attached at the back. Pick a theme, for example famous actresses. You could also, depending on the crowd, be a bit naughty and have the words related to – ahem – marital life. As the guests mingle, ask them to try and figure out the anagrams as they move around. It breaks the ice and gives everyone a giggle.

Kiss and Tell

All seasoned wives have their tales to tell and this activity can really produce some great laughs for everybody, especially if the ladies present know each other for many years. Stories can be funny or naughty: this game is more or less a variation on the theme of 'my most embarrassing moment'.

The Silliest Thing My Husband Ever Did

This is one of those games that only more mature women will enjoy, as they'll all know one another (and everybody's husbands) long enough to appreciate the joke, while being sensible about exactly how bad the confessions get! 'I'll never forget the day that we were late for wee Seán's Holy Communion and my car wouldn't start, while my hubby's was already in for a service. He decided that it was brake fluid that was my problem and was so angry at me for not having taken care of it myself. He came storming back from the tool shed and walloped this mad-looking green stuff into my brake fluid holder. When I looked at the label on the bottle, it was anti-freeze…' Well, there are many variations on the theme but these kinds of stories give everyone a chance to unwind and laugh at the stresses and strains of marriage, while wishing the new, golden bride a wonderful new life.

Party Piece

Party pieces are something we don't see much of any more but there are plenty of ladies out there who would be only too glad to wow us with their piano-playing or shock us with their Barbara Streisand impersonations. Before the henparty, ask all the guests to prepare a party piece for the night. The best performance is picked by the Hen and wins a small prize.

> When my older sister came out with the bombshell that she was going to get married, a few months short of her fifty-fifth birthday, we were all delighted. But as you can imagine, my younger sister and I weren't too sure what to do with her. But she's a brilliant cook and she worked as a home economics teacher for most of her career. So we decided to do a 'pot luck' evening in the house of one of her friends and invited each of the guests to cook a dish that she might have taught them, or given them the recipe for down the years. Then we asked everybody to try and remember which year she would have given them the recipe and to remember a story from that time. So when we served dinner there was a ready-made opportunity for fun, because everybody had an anecdote that related to the cooking and to her life.
>
> *Trudy*

> When I remarried about ten years after separating from my first husband, most of my friends were as excited at the idea of a henparty as anything else. A bit beyond the red devil-horns stage, we'd still be into

stilettos and dressing up, so I organised a Saturday night stay-over in one of those lovely country houses that run B&Bs. It was just outside Wexford town, so we did a gallery walkabout in the afternoon, cocktails at one of the better bars in town, theatre at the Arts Centre and then back to the big house, where we sat out at a big wooden table in the garden telling stories and singing – and flirting with the dishy Polish waiter – until the early hours. It was fantastic.

Caroline

10

Money Matters

So far, we have touched on all the major elements of the henparty: where to go and where to stay; the afternoon activity; the meal and dressing up; the games; and finally pubbing and clubbing. But the one important question remains: who pays for what and how are costs shared? This is an age-old problem for Hens or maids of honour who may not know the procedure, or may be nervous of how to approach the topic of money.

The biggest dilemma for a henparty organiser is whether the bridesmaids and maid of honour should pay for all the dressing-up gear, or whether the guests should be asked to pay for their own. Who pays for the Hen herself, or does she pay a portion? How is the bill broken down? Should everyone split the costs for everything that is organised?

There are no hard and fast rules and every situation is different but there are a few basic points that should be considered when approaching henparty finances. It is an area that should be organised every bit as carefully as the rest of the henparty, since lack of clarity where finances are concerned can be embarrassing or even disastrous.

Twenty-plus women on a night out is an expensive affair and henparty organisers have frequently been left short because of a lack of planning.

When organising a henparty, we think it's best to ensure that the costs are evenly distributed and proportionate to the level at which a guest is taking part. If the guest isn't going on the afternoon activity, don't ask them to pay a sum including that cost. For instance if you have a bellydancing class organised and three girls can't make it, don't ask them to pay anyway. You would be surprised how many do!

In terms of the dressing up gear, there are two options:

1. Tell the guests what to buy and ask them to bring the selected gear along with them on the night. This isn't always the smartest move, however, as people may not buy the correct props, or may not have time to get them at all. The whole theme may flop. Instead of buying a short, pink wig and a white boa, a lazy guest may scupper the whole plan and buy a long, pink wig and a pink boa.
2. Buy all the gear yourself or with the bridesmaids or other relatives of the bride, make sure that you receive payment from each guest beforehand for their gear and distribute it at the henparty. There is a common misconception that the maid of honour or the bridesmaids should take the hit for the whole cost. This is simply not the case. Most women realise the expense involved and will be only too happy to pay their own way. Nobody in

this day and age expects any one person to pay for twenty bunny rabbit outfits or twenty feather boas.

In terms of paying for the Hen's gear, there is no reason why this can't also be divided among the rest of the guests. It will add a couple of euro for each person at most. Some maids of honour or close relatives prefer to pay for this particular expense themselves and that is fine too. In general the Hen should not pay for anything on her big night – the meal, the drinks or even her accommodation. Most women are happy to chip in for the Hen or, as with the dressing up gear, some maids of honour or sisters will cover the Hen themselves.

METHODS OF COLLECTING MONEY

Some henparty organisers are über-efficient and terribly clever when it comes to cash. These ladies will organise the henparty and then sit down and work out what it will cost. This cost will cover activities, dressing-up gear, accommodation, drinks and meals. They will then divide the total by the number of guests and as each person arrives at the henparty they pay the maid of honour, or whoever is organising the henparty.

The thinking behind this method is that guests don't have to put their hands in their pockets for the rest of the night. Everything has been taken care of and if there is money left over it can go on another round of drinks. It's a good idea in theory but only if all the guests are going to be participating in exactly the same elements of the henparty. People do drink at different speeds, so using the 'rounds' method to buy drinks can slow down or speed up drinking for some guests who may prefer (or be better off) drinking at their own pace.

Another method of organising money is to pay it into a bank account before the big day. Yes, cold and calculating as it may seem, some women do send on bank details when they are organising henparties and ask for a predetermined amount of money to be lodged. As already described, this money will cover all the costs associated with the henparty. This would be essential if the henparty is being held abroad, for example. Or if the maid of honour is a control freak.

While these procedures are both valid, one of the most popular methods of money management on a henparty is still to 'pay as you go'. The quad-bikers, bellydancers and hat-makers all pay for themselves after their respective activities. When the meal is over and the bill is split, everyone present pays their portion. In terms of the dressing up gear, the henparty organiser asks everyone just before the meal for reimbursement of money paid out on the paraphernalia. The guests pay for drinks in the pub and for their accommodation as they leave on the last day. Simple.

Paying afterwards is also an option. Many henparty organisers will wait until everyone is leaving and ask them for reimbursement for the meal, accommodation and everything else. This method is the least popular, since people can leave early, lose their wallet, put off payment 'until tomorrow' or longer, and chances are that the organisers will get caught out with a hefty bill. However well-intentioned the guests may be on the night, it's very hard to recoup money afterwards.

Yes, I was asked to a henparty where the organiser asked us to lodge money to her bank account. I thought it was off. I mean, you can't really be asking people to put money into an account when we didn't even know what it was going to cost. I wasn't the only one who wasn't impressed with this but nobody said anything and we lodged the money. We ended up having to give more the morning after the henparty which, to be honest, only made matters worse.

Lorraine

The sneakiest thing I ever saw on a henparty was where the bridesmaid worked her share of the price of the bedroom into the costs of the bride so we all ended up paying for the bridesmaid who shared a room with the bride. I just thought it was so cheeky.

Anne

11

Nice Ideas

I cannot repeat often enough that the whole point of a henparty is to celebrate the Hen and make her feel special. Pull out all the stops to focus full attention on the Hen, giving her the send-off she will never forget. We have covered the basic henparty elements but there are some additional gestures that don't have to cost the earth, don't have to take a lot of time to organise but can make the Hen feel she has the best friends in the world. We call them 'nice ideas'. The first nice idea is worth considering a given, even if you take or leave the others.

A HENPARTY MEMORY BOOK

This personal touch is not just an option for the henparty, it is a must. Nothing but *nothing* else could ever evoke the same emotional reaction as this. Prepare yourself for tears and general hysteria as the henparty memory book is handed over. The beauty of this nice idea is that it is simple and usually inexpensive, yet it is something the Hen will have forever.

In essence, the henparty memory book is a scrapbook, notebook or collection of messages, photos, stories and memories from all the guests at the henparty. It combines messages of good luck and best wishes with stories from the past and advice for the future. Everyone can get involved and even those who aren't able to attend the henparty can add their message to the memory book.

The basic book can be a photo album, scrap book or notebook. An A4 size is best but use your own judgement. You can decorate the book with stickers and glitter, or leave it plain. Custom-made books are available in some shops, though not as elaborate as the ones you make yourself.

Before the henparty, ask each of the guests to write a message to the Hen. Hand-written is best as it is more personal but for those overseas or far away, an email is fine. The content of the message is completely down to each individual. Some tell stories of the Hen from years before, or remind her of old boyfriends and love interests. Some give words of advice on marriage and what to expect. Others include photos to bring back memories of dodgy haircuts and horrendous fashion. What all the messages have in common is that each is a personal message from a friend, sister, mother or relative to the Hen on her very special day.

The notebook can be partly prepared in advance with the Hen's name and date already written on the inside cover and the names of the guests expected, along with the location of the henparty. As the guests arrive, the organiser discreetly takes their entries from them. It is then simply a matter of gluing them into the notebook, and interspersing them with the photos. It is also a nice idea to write a note beside each photo, giving the name of the person who provided it.

It is usual to present henparty memory books to Hens at the meal but use your own discretion. It's always best to present the book before the Hen has had too many drinkies because she may be liable to bawl her head off with emotion, or lose the book itself. The henparty memory book is a beautiful keepsake for the Hen, which she will have for years to come. It adds an emotional moment to the evening, between the vodka and the champagne. If you like the idea of getting a henparty memory book made professionally, there are companies in the marketplace that are happy to do it for you.

If you only have time to organise one nice idea, let this be it. For the henparty planner with a little time on her hands, however, the range of extras that will make your henparty even more special is extensive.

Here are some of our favourites:

A LAMINATED PLACE-MAT

Shame the Hen, while also creating some 'Awww' moments: have laminated place-mats made for the henparty meal. Firstly, dig out old some photos of the Hen from down through the years. Next, scan them, or have them scanned into a digital format and cut and paste them into a nice arrangement on an A4 sheet. Most computers these days have scanning facilities and even a small desktop publishing programme to enable you to do this. Print a copy for everyone at the henparty meal and have it laminated at a printing shop. When you arrive at the restaurant, either ask the waiting staff to put the mats out at each place setting or do it yourself.

The photos will be a great ice-breaker at the meal, as well as a funny way to embarrass the Hen!

A PHOTO COLLAGE

Another effective way to get right to the Hen's heart is with a photo collage, which is a slight variation on the henparty memory book. Ask everyone who is going to be at the henparty to send you some old photos of the Hen. If there are ladies from all different areas of the Hen's life, you should get an excellent selection – work, school, college. Simply buy an A3 picture frame and arrange the photos in it. It's nice to add a heading as well, something to mark the occasion, like the Hen's name and the date of the henparty. You can present the collage to the Hen at the meal.

A RADIO REQUEST

Some nice ideas cost only a few cent but can make a girl feel like the most loved babe in the world. On the way to the henparty, phone a radio station and ask them to play a request for the Hen. Liaise with the other cars to make sure everyone is listening. The Hen will feel like a million dollars – all for the price of a phone call.

'THIS IS YOUR LIFE'

This nice idea requires a little more effort than the others but if it is carried out effectively, it can have the room in tears. The *This is Your Life* idea is basically a mock-up of the old television show. It's a book describing the life of the Hen to date. Simply take a scrapbook and using some nice red wrapping paper, cover the book and write/

type/stick the words 'This is Your Life' on the front. For the early years, talk to the Hen's family and old school friends. Collect as many photos and stories as you can and add them to the book. Move on to the secondary school stage and do the same thing. Type up the stories, add them to the book and stick in the photos. Include milestones, places and people, for example: 'Mary started school in St Brigid's on 5 September 1983 and her first teacher was Sr Anne.' A photo to accompany each milestone would be great. Continue up to the present day, including college, work, birthdays and other celebrations. On the night of the henparty, stand up and announce to the Hen, 'This Is Your Life.' Select some milestones to read out to the table. Pass the book around afterwards for everyone to see the pictures. This is a lovely nice idea for a friend or sister and although it takes a bit of time, it is well worth the effort involved.

A CHAMPAGNE LUNCH

Another simple yet effective nice idea is to spoil the Hen with a champagne lunch on the way to the henparty. If you are travelling to your location by bus or mini-bus, ask the driver to pull over at an attractive picnic area and get everyone out. If you are travelling by car, ask everyone to meet at a specific spot along the way. Pass around plastic cups or plastic champagne flutes and after popping the cork, propose a toast to the Hen. If you want to blow the budget, get a couple of bottles of Veuve Cliquot or Moët et Chandon; but a bottle of sparkling pear cider at about a quarter of the price can achieve the very same effect. Strawberries and nibbles are an added touch for this nice idea. Once again, the bride will feel she's the centre of the universe.

A SMALL GIFT

Ask each of the guests to bring a small gift for the Hen, something that reminds them of her, or a time in their lives that they shared with her. Put a price limit on the gift, as it is the thought that is important here, not the cost of the present. Put all the gifts in a basket or a box and at some point in the day, ask the Hen to pull them out one by one and guess who they are from. This will generate some further touching 'Awww' moments.

AN AUTOGRAPHED T-SHIRT

This is another simple, nice idea and the Hen will have it for ever. It's relatively inexpensive and doesn't take a lot of time to organise. Get a T-shirt custom-printed for the henparty. Most T-shirt printers will do this for you. Text such as 'Tracy's Hen, July 2009' is usual, although this is completely at your own discretion. At the henparty, produce the T-shirt and ask everyone present to sign it with a black marker and leave a small message for the Hen. Indelible ink is best for obvious reasons. It's a really nice idea for the Hen and despite the small cost and effort that is required, the Hen will get a great kick out of it. One really flashy variation would be to frame the T-shirt afterwards so that the Hen can hang it in her downstairs loo.

A DVD OF PHOTOS

This nice idea is a more modern take on the collage of photos. The basic idea behind it is to make a DVD of photos of the Hen and play it either at the meal or at another stage of the henparty. Scan as many photos of the Hen as you can find. Involve the other guests and ask the Hen's family for some. Burn the images onto to a DVD and set it to music. The techies among you will be rubbing your hands in glee at the thought of this project. For the technophobes, there are companies that will make the DVDs for you if you send them the pictures. The guests will be impressed and the Hen will love the trip down memory lane the DVD will provide.

SOMETHING BORROWED, SOMETHING BLUE

If the Hen hasn't already decided on her 'something old, something new, something borrowed, something blue', give her suitable items in a nice box at the henparty. You could rope in some older family members for this nice idea and talk to those closest to the Hen. She doesn't have to use them on the big day, so don't get too worried about getting it spot-on, but it's a simple gesture that will mean a lot. For example if her 'something new' is her wedding dress, why not put a little picture of a wedding dress in the box. 'Something old' could be a gift her mother or grandmother is giving her.

If you would prefer not to talk to her family, it could just be a gift from the girls. 'Something old' could be a picture from school; 'something new' could be a nice photo frame; 'something borrowed' could be a book for the honeymoon; 'something blue' could be a garter. What ever items you decide on, it's a touching nice idea.

THE BOTTOM DRAWER

The idea of the bottom drawer has been dying away and we think it should definitely be revived! The term is hundreds of years old. It has its origins in the tradition whereby whenever a lady received an expensive present before her wedding, it would be stored in the bottom drawer of her chest of drawers, along with all her valuables. Back then, these would have included table-cloths and silver spoons. Today many aunts and grannies still give a Hen a set of silver spoons, table linen or bed linen and tell her they are for her bottom drawer. On a henparty it's nice to have a bottom drawer moment. A budget limit can be set and you don't have to stick to tablecloths.

THE TROUSSEAU

We must point out that the bottom drawer is not to be confused with the trousseau! The trousseau is a term that once referred to the bride's entire outfit – her veil, dress and shoes. Today, some older relatives and friends might give the bride a nice set of briefs or a negligée 'for her trousseau' with a sly wink and a little giggle. But like the bottom drawer, this custom is dying out and we feel it should be revived! Ask everyone at the henparty to being a small gift for the Hen's trousseau, such as nice pairs of panties, nighties or innocent gifts for the Hen to take on her honeymoon.

I still have the book that the girls gave me at my henparty. I take it out every so often and read all the notes. I was so happy when they gave it to me. It meant so much that they had all gone to trouble to write me a message. There was even one from my mum as well as pictures she had put in from when I was small. It was just perfect.

Sheila

For my henparty, my sister got a video camera and carried it with her everywhere for the month beforehand. Whenever she met someone who knew me, she would ask them to say a few words to me to wish me well. My uncles were on it, my old English teacher, my boss. What was really special was the last person on the video was my fiancé, who told me he hoped I had a great night and said he loved me so much and couldn't wait to marry me. I was crying, my sister was crying and half my friends were crying.

Veronica

12

THE KITCHEN PARTY

Many Hens underestimate the value of having a kitchen party before their wedding and many more don't even know what a kitchen party is! We cannot stress enough how much fun a kitchen party can be, how many awkward situations it can help you avoid and how many great presents the Hen will get from it. This chapter is a step-by-step guide to the kitchen party.

WHAT IS A KITCHEN PARTY?
Before the sexual liberation of women in the 1960s, it was the men who had all the fun and got to have a night on the town before they got married. As described in Chapter One, the men were free to paint the town red and enjoy their last night of freedom with booze, music and all the boys. Ladies, on the other hand, enjoyed cups of tea and chats at their neighbours' or aunts' houses. While it hardly seems fair, this was the norm and these gatherings became known as 'kitchen parties'.

The present-day kitchen party is slightly different to the kitchen parties of the 1950s. Kitchen parties were hugely popular in the 1980s and 1990s but are not as commonplace today because many ladies simply aren't aware of them and don't realise their merits.

To begin with, a kitchen party is a gathering of very close friends (the inner circle): mothers, mothers-in-law, aunts, grandmothers, neighbours, old family friends and any other females who aren't from school, college or work. Kitchen parties always have a great sense of nostalgia, with several generations in attendance. There aren't a lot of mini-skirts and boob tubes at a kitchen party. Instead, there are laughs, hugs, words of wisdom and a great sense of family and place.

The reason they are called kitchen parties is that all the guests bring a present for the Hen for her kitchen. The original thinking was that these gifts would help her become the 'best wife' she could possibly be. Rolling pins, aprons, pastry bags and Tupperware were the most common presents in those days, not to mention a few good saucepans – and we all know the value of a good saucepan in the kitchen. This tradition continues today with similar presents being given, although thankfully with less emphasis on their making a 'better wife' out of the bride.

The kitchen party is traditionally held outside the Hen's mother's house, unless absolutely necessary. It is usually held in an aunt's house, or a neighbour's, or the home of a close female friend of the family. It is held quite close to the wedding, typically within two to three weeks of the Big Day. A large spread is put in place, with sandwiches, crisps, dips and all sorts of hors d'oeuvres. Some hostesses will go so far as to cook hot food, though this really isn't necessary. Drinks vary hugely, from tea and coffee to soft drinks, to wine and beer and even to spirits. The norm, however, is usually wine in terms of alcoholic drinks.

Guests arrive and leave their presents in a basket by the door. A limit is usually put on the price of presents, typically ten or twenty Euro. After a few cups of tea and a couple of glasses of wine, proceedings begin. The Hen sits in the middle of the room and is blindfolded and someone is on hand with a notebook and pen. The Hen is handed the presents one by one and she must guess by feeling the present what each one is and who gave it to her. The person with the notebook records all the lines the Hen uses in her descriptions. Once all the presents are open, the comments are read back to the group with the opening line: 'What "Sarah" will say to "David" on her wedding night.' The Hen is suitably shamed! For example if she is handed a rolling pin all wrapped up and comments, 'It's a weird shape,' or, 'It's very long,' this gets the laugh when read out loud afterwards. The book is then given to the Hen and a nice touch is to get everyone at the kitchen party to sign it.

Once the present-opening is over, ladies play games, tell stories or have another drink. It's all completely down to the discretion of the hostess. Kitchen parties can often last long into the night, with the older relatives surprising everyone with their sly innuendoes and double entendres!

REASONS TO HAVE A KITCHEN PARTY
Kitchen parties are a great idea and great fun. There is nothing better than sitting with all your female relatives

and having a good old-fashioned giggle. There aren't too many occasions when all the generations of the females of a family will be together, so kitchen parties are nights that memories are made of. With close family friends in attendance as well, it is simply a lovely evening for everyone coming up to the wedding.

Another reason to have a kitchen party is that it is a good-value night out. Apart from the wine and nibbles, kitchen parties are very cost-effective. It's not like the showing off and the glitz of the henparty. It's just about the laughs and the memories. There's no pressure in terms of showing the girls how it's done or impressing the ladies at work. In fact, the more modest the kitchen party, the more laughs you'll have.

Kitchen parties are another way to create a memorable build-up to the wedding for the Hen. This is another night to look forward to, another night of spoiling her and making her feel everyone thinks she is special.

Finally, one of the most important reasons to have a kitchen party is that everyone can get involved. In Chapter 2, we addressed the problem of asking older relatives to the henparty. Having a kitchen party solves this dilemma. The Hen is free to have her crazy henparty and all the trimmings, as well as having another fun night where the mothers, aunts and grannies can send her off but without the danger of their being offended by strippers and willy drinking straws.

The guests, on this occasion, are the women and girls who are members of the Hen's family, as well as older family friends and neighbours who have known her all her life. They will also want to send her off before her big day and feel they are part of the proceedings. Having a kitchen party allows this to happen, giving the Hen a unique chance to celebrate with her closest family members in an intimate and comfortable setting.

Back then, the kitchen party was organised by one of the bridesmaids as one of her main duties – so my sister organised mine. This was one of the highlights of the pre-wedding period, since in those days there were no 'afters' on the wedding day. The kitchen party brought together all the friends, work colleagues, neighbours and particularly cousins to one celebration. Everyone brought something small for the kitchen. All gifts were very welcome, because in those days people didn't live together before marriage. All the presents were carefully wrapped and the bride had to sit on the floor in the middle of a circle and feel each parcel, to try and guess its contents. All the while, someone was writing down the comments made by the bride as she did this. The comments were then read out loud to the party as if they were what was said between the newlyweds! As you can imagine, there were a few blushes and a lot of laughs. I remember feeling like the belle of the ball. I still use a marble-handled cake slice that I received that night and wonder where Cora – the girl who gave it to me – is now. After thirty-six years, the memory of that joy is still in my heart.

Patricia

A kitchen party was my mother's suggestion. I didn't take it seriously but in the end, just to please her, I said OK. Because my bridesmaid was busy organising my henparty, Mum said her sister would love to host it and that it would be a good idea for my relatives to have a bit of fun as they wouldn't be going to the henparty. The night started with a few glasses of wine and everyone mingled. Then I had to feel all the presents and guess their contents. My mum was shocked at how much the presents had changed since her kitchen party. I got some nice pieces of pottery and glass and someone said they were like mini-wedding presents. We had great fun when the comments were read out and there were some pretty wild responses from my aunts that I couldn't believe! We had pizza then and some more wine and told stories until late. It was a great night and I'm really glad Mum talked me into it.

Una

Conclusion

A henparty means something different to everyone. Some women love the traditional night on the tiles, others prefer to be pampered at a spa for the weekend. Some women choose a quiet meal with a few friends, others book weeks away in Spain or weekends in London. There are many, many options available to today's bride. But no matter how a bride marks her last night as a single woman with her friends, the event is still known as a henparty. It is a gathering of women before the wedding and a celebration of the bride, of family, of friendship, memories and good times to come.

Over the last ten years, henparties have changed dramatically. What was once a low key, one-night affair has evolved into a mini-event requiring almost as much planning and originality as the wedding itself, with probably as much excitement. Ten years ago women were happy to have a few drinks and a dance locally but the contemporary henparty has evolved into much more and its organisation must reflect that. As we have seen throughout the course of this book, henparties today can be elaborate, artistic, city- or country-based, active, pampering or simply wild.

Despite recent economic changes, this henparty

tradition is now firmly established and there is definitely no going back. If budget is an issue, imagination becomes the order of the day and so research, innovation and a bit of good old-fashioned preparation are all the more necessary.

What hasn't changed as the henparty has evolved is that from start to finish the occasion must always be about the Hen. Whether what you plan is quiet, crazy or classy, the Hen must always be the focal point of the event. Whatever tips you may have picked up from this book, we can only hope you have appreciated the most important point of all – *it's always all about the Hen*. Even the most horrendous 'Hen-zilla' deserves the best henparty possible.

Love them or hate them, henparties are here to stay as an integral part of the wedding process. So no matter how much you hate wearing flashing bunny ears, or paintballing for the tenth time, grin and bear it because when your turn comes, you'll ask them to do it too. And they will…

ABOUT THE AUTHOR

Kate Hyde grew up in County Cork and graduated from UCC with a degree in Business Information Systems. After college, Kate worked in both Accounting and IT before finally realising her dream and starting her own business, www.henparty.ie, in 2008.

Since then, the website has grown from strength to strength and led to Kate's successful appearance on the first series of the Irish *Dragons' Den*. Kate was the first female entrepreneur to secure investment from two of the Irish dragons, Gavin Duffy and Niall O'Farrell.

Kate is currently expanding this flourishing venture and working on the development of several other business ideas. In her spare time she likes to read, run and take art classes. Kate lives with her husband in Waterford.